The Old Rebel

A life in Nuneaton

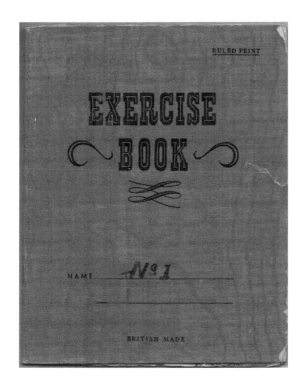

By George Leonard Clarke

1885-1960

.

George and Gertie Clarke

Nov 14th, 1940

Contents

Acknowledgements

Preparing this book would not have been possible without the generous help of:

Gertie's nephew Leonard Brooks (son of Levi Brooks), Gertie's niece Joan Wells (daughter of Percy Brooks), and in particular Gertie's niece Doreen Thomas (known as Dean, daughter of Gertie's sister Mabel, one of most engaging characters in the book), for her sparkling company and some of the loveliest family pictures.

George's youngest daughter Audrey's children (Stella Mercer, Robert Sheehan, and Michael Sheehan), for rescuing many family photographs when College Street was sold in 2004. Tom Betteridge's wife Heather for supplying many pictures, including the lovely ones of Norah's wedding.

Whoever collated the Photographic Coronation Souvenir in 1902 for the coronation of Edward VII, held in Nuneaton Library. David Floyd, for the picture of the Crystal Palace Smoke Room.

Ruth Sidwell for her painstaking editing, love, support, and cups of tea.

And last but not least, Peter Lee, who is the Chairman of the Nuneaton and North Warwickshire Family History Society. Peter was very generous in his support during the preparation of the book, and in allowing the use of his extensive library of pictures and resources. His knowledge and enthusiasm for all things connected with Nuneaton is endless and invaluable. If that wasn't enough, Peter is also the best company you could wish for, and rekindles your belief in the value and joy of family and community.

Editor's Introduction

This book was written by my Grandad, George Clarke: the story of his life in Nuneaton. It was written in fountain pen in his beautiful copperplate handwriting, between July 1956 and January 1957. The nine school exercise books (red, ruled feint) were kept in a red cardboard box under the shoes and handbags in the bottom of Mum's wardrobe until she died in 2000.

I was four years old when George died, and I only have one memory of him, sitting by the piano in the front room at 183 College Street, offering me a fruit pastille. His walking stick leaned against the wall: he needed it following a roof fall in the Nuneaton Colliery, which left his right leg over an inch shorter than his left.

My brother Tom was born in 1943, and so knew him very well. During the 2000s we talked many times about writing a commentary on the book, but Tom sadly and suddenly died in September 2010, taking his memories with him.

By all accounts George was great company. I hope you enjoy reading his story as much as I do.

David Sidwell
January 2011

Editor's Note

George's words are set in Bookman Old Style, 10 point (other text, such as this Note, is set in in Calibri). From the scanned pages of the original books, you can see that George's writing is naturally fluent, with few corrections. The only editorial changes are to split the text into more logical sequences, and break up long sentences.

For the technically curious amongst you George's 72,262 words were dictated using the Dragon Naturally Speaking voice recognition software. Despite its trouble with period words (such as wagonettes), and understandable hopelessness with good old Midlands phrases (like well-britched), reading the text out loud was much quicker than typing it all in (or became so once system memory was upgraded to 4GB, anyway).

The footnotes are mine, to add relevant family details, and explain historical events, abbreviations, pre-decimal currency, and imperial weights. The pictures have been collected from all around the family, and have been inserted where they best fit with the text, even though this means some periods are far better represented than others.

If you have any photographs that would sit well in the book, or would like to recommend a change to the text, please let me know by email: theoldrebel@davidsidwell.co.uk

First Edition published November 2011.

ISBN Number 978 1 849 140867

Orderable from the Nuneaton and North Warwickshire Family History Society www.nnwfhs.org.uk or from www.completelynovel.co.uk.

List of Illustrations

Foreword by Peter Lee, Chairman, Nuneaton and North Warwickshire Family History Society

As a student of old Nuneaton I see a lot of archive material and memorabilia. I enjoy it all, but rarely do I read anything as good as this memoir, the life of an ordinary working man, George Clarke.

This is just about as good as it gets. It isn't a diary, but a well written, lively and interesting account of his life, his precious memories, and the colourful incidents which, without his endeavours, would be lost to eternity.

Can I make a plea to everyone reading this to record your memories for posterity as George has done. He is a role model for local historians. His was not the big world of business and high finance, but that of a hard working man, who did the best for himself and his family. His account brings flooding back those glorious years we can only just remember today, of a straight- forward world with no political correctness, where people instinctively did the right thing, struggled to overcome adversity, applied common sense, and enjoyed themselves despite their modest aspirations. He knew what was right and wrong, and tells us about it; and he helped and respected others through good times and bad.

He also sets an example for most people in the sense that they feel their lives are so ordinary as not to be worth putting down on paper. The way he carefully observes the incidents in his life and narrates that story shows that it can be done. And when it is done well, as he has here, then his world comes alive again.

We as local and family historians often try to think where our hobby will take us. That magical elusive place has been reached here by George and we should all follow his lead in delineating the story of our lives for the benefit of future generations.

Peter Lee

The Old Rebel

A life in Nuneaton

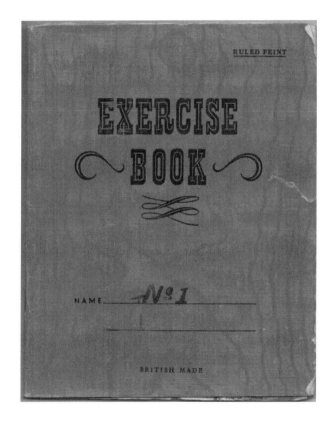

By George Leonard Clarke

1885-1960

Title and Dedication page

FRIDAY, JULY 13:/56.

TITLE. "THE OLD REBEL".
By G. L. Clarke.

DEDICATION.

To my "best pal", my "Little Lady", my wife,
Who "passed on" Dec: 4th 1955.
It was one of the things that she always
wanted me to, & so, in memory of a
lady, in the real sense of the word, I
have tried to show, in this book, how happy
we always were, when we were together.
Her love, charm, sincerity, tolerance, & Courage
inspired me to overcome numerous setbacks
& disappointments, & when things went wrong,
through strikes & accidents, she never
grumbled, or blamed me, we fought side by
side, made the best of life, & carried on.
If there is a life "here after", I know she
will be waiting for me, & sometime, perhaps,
we shall be together again, I sincerely hope so.

Dedication

To my best pal, my Little Lady, my wife, who 'passed on' December 4th, 1955.

It was one of the things that she always wanted me to do and so, in the memory of a lady, in the _real_ sense of the word, I have tried to show in this book how happy we always were when we were together.

Her love, charm, sincerity, tolerance, and courage inspired me to overcome numerous setbacks and disappointments, and when things went wrong, through strikes and accidents, she never grumbled or blamed me, we fought side by side, made the best of life, and carried on.

If there is a life 'here after', I know she will be waiting for me, and sometime perhaps, we shall be together again, I sincerely hope so.

Foreword

This is the story of an ordinary working man's life. The members of my family, and my wife (before her death six months ago) were always urging me to write my life story, so as I always have plenty of spare time now, I thought I would please them, and I hope they will not be disappointed when they have read it and come to the end.

I have had a wonderful life, full of love, joy and sorrow, ups and downs, changes, and have worked in many different trades and businesses. It has been a very hard road at times, dull and tedious, but very interesting most of the time, and I always really enjoy tackling a fresh job, it was always my aim to thoroughly master all details and get on top of the work.

During my working life, the period of over 50 years, I have met all sorts and grades of people, as my memory is very good, I can remember most of the incidents that happened during that time.

For over 55 years, my wife (my best pal) was always with me, heart and soul, and I shall never forget how she encouraged me when things looked black or went wrong. Her love, patience, tolerance, and courage helped me many a time, when the struggle to earn a living was sometimes very hard and difficult in the 'good old days', before the Labour Party were strong enough to obtain better conditions.

Those who read this book will find some of the statements hard to digest, especially some of the youthful members of the present generation, as, (owing to the constant repetition of the glories of the Conservative

Party and private enterprise, by the National Press of the Country, which, by the way, is in control of more than 90% of the Daily and Weekly newspapers), they think all the big wages and good conditions have been brought about by the Tories.

I hope it will interest every reader, man or woman, I know it will give you something to think about, some good laughs, and perhaps, a few tears.

I only hope when you have read it, you will weigh matters up, and decide which form of government is best for the majority of the population of this country, if you want a good future for your children, I know what your decision will be.

George Leonard Clarke

Nuneaton, July 13th, 1956

First page of Book 1

Chapter No 1.

I was born 70 years ago, in 1885, at the little village of Waligrove on Sowe, near the village school & Wykin Colliery, where my father was the Under-Manager, his wages were just over 30/- per week, & my mother did her best to increase the income by working a hand-loom, weaving ribbon, in her spare time, the pay was not much, but it helped out.

There were no striking incidents that I could remember, as by the time when I was four years of age, my father had a terrible row, with the Colliery Manager, & packed his job up, & we moved to Nuneaton.

The only incidents about the Colliery I learnt later on, listening to my father talking to one of his friends, he said that the Colliery output of coal all went to Coventry by Coal carts, or by boats on the Canal to different parts of the Country, there was no Railway at that time connected with the Colliery, so that during the winter time when the roads were bad (& they were bad in those days,) & the Canal frozen over, there was no work for the miners, & many a week, they drew no wages at all, & as my dad said, "they went hungry to —— many a day" (3)

Chapter 1

I was born 70 years ago, in 1885, at the little village of Walsgrave-on-Sowe, near the village school and Wykin Colliery, where my father was the Under Manager, his wages were just over 30 shillings per week, and my mother did her best to increase the income by working a hand-loom, weaving ribbon, in her spare time, the pay was not much, but it helped out[1].

There were no striking incidents that I could remember, as by the time when I was four years of age, my father had a terrible row with the colliery manager, packed his job up, and we moved to Nuneaton.

The only incidents about the colliery I learned later on, listening to my father talking to one of his friends. He said that the colliery output of all coal went to Coventry by coal carts, or by boats on the Canal, to different parts of the country. There was no railway at that time connected with the Colliery, so that during the winter time when the roads were bad (and they were bad in those days) and the Canal frozen over, there was no work for the miners, and many a week, they drew no wages at all, and as my Dad said "they went hungry too – many a day". The miners were allowed 'allowance coal', the condition was that they were allowed to take as much as they could carry off the pit-bank on the top of their heads.

Incidentally, a few years after my father left, the same Colliery Manager who fell out with my Dad tied himself to a tree in his orchard, and blew himself to bits with a heavy charge of dynamite. Dad had a few drinks extra that night when he heard the news.

---

[1] *George's father was Thomas Clarke 1851-1931, born in Nuneaton. His mother was Ellen Pickering, 1853-1922, born in Brailes, near Shipston-on-Stour.*

23

Dad, Mother and all the family, nine of us all together, moved to Nuneaton, then a very small town, to a very small house in Princes Street, and my dad got employed at Stanley's Cold Pit (which closed down about the year 1900).

Workers at Stanley's Cold Pit, c. 1895

While he was there, there was a vacancy for an Under-Manager at Number 5 Griff Colliery, for which he applied, and was appointed (Metz Pit, they call it, as it was sunk during the siege of Metz in Lovaine, France).

We moved from Nuneaton to a small house in Chilvers Coton and from there to a very nice house in Arbury Road, Stockingford, where we stayed several years. I think that this was one of the happiest periods of my life, as a good many incidents happened there which had some influence on my later life.

Chapter 2

My schooldays began, and I attended Heath End Infants School.

The School-Mistress was a rather stern looking spinster, Miss Clifton, who was a very strict disciplinarian, and would not tolerate any nonsense or unruly behaviour. We were taught the three Rs[2], singing, and one third of the total school hours time was taken up by Scripture lessons. These were rammed home by the teachers, the Vicar of Chilvers Coton Church, and his curate.

**Miss Clifton, and Rev. R Chadwick
Headmistress, Heath End Mixed School,
and Vicar of Chilvers Coton Church, 1902**

The Vicar was a very gentle quietly spoken man, completely dominated by his wife, who remarked to one of the prominent members of the Church, "Robert ought to have been I, and I ought to have been Robert, we might get something done then."

The Coton Church 'living' was under the patronage of the Newdegate Family, and our school was a Church School, and came in the same category. General Sir Edward

---

[2] *Reading, 'riting, and 'rithmetic*

Newdegate was in residence at Arbury Hall at that time, he was always on horseback when he came to visit the school, and we all had to stand to attention while he was in the room. I never saw him take any notice of any of the children.

Lieut.-General Sir Edward Newdegate KCB, 1902

Miss Clifton was always very kind to me, and when I got to the upper classes, I ran all the errands for her, to Nuneaton two or three times a week, and to Arbury Hall twice a week, with reports and requests etc. I was a fairly good scholar and could always keep up with the rest of the class, so that the time spent running errands did not affect my position in the class, I was usually at the top, ("Big Head"). There was nothing unusual happened, plenty of fun, scraps, and 'jitters' when the Government Inspector came to conduct the examinations.

I made friends with a lad named Frank Beck when I was about nine years old, he was attending the Bablake

Secondary School, and his influence had some bearing on my later life. He taught me boxing, chess, and as he was a little superior in the social scale to the majority of my schoolmates, I naturally copied him, and thus improved my vocabulary and general behaviour.

His father was the Chief Engineer for Messrs Stanley Brothers Brickworks and Collieries, and we used to roam all about the brick yards and fields belonging to the Company.

Stanley's Colliery, 1890's

We always had a terrier with us, (it belonged to Frank's elder brother), named Peter, what a game little fellow he was. The brick-yards were full of stray cats, some of them big and fierce as Tigers, and the terrier was always chasing them, and got scratched and badly bitten many times, but he was already in waiting for us to start out 'on the trail'.

Our house had a lovely garden, two lovely out-houses, a big verandah all across the back of the building, where we could play when it was snowing or raining. Later on we had a very big pig sty, all wood, which we would use as a playroom when it had been cleaned and lime-washed. When we first had the pig sty Mother bought two young pigs, bought all the feeding stuff, and reared them until they were very nice 'bacon pigs'. She intended to sell one to the Butcher, to provide 'extras' for Christmas, and have the other one killed and then 'cured' for Ham and Bacon to last all through the winter, but my dad got in first, one day when Mother was out visiting, he sold one to the Butcher, and stuck to the money. Mother played 'hell-up' with him, and that was the finish of pig keeping.

At the bottom of the garden, there was a rather good quickthorn hedge and a semi-filled up ditch which was overhung by the hedge. The field beyond belonged to the local Butcher, who was a farmer in a small way as well, and had several hundreds of fowl, some of these hens used to come and lay their eggs in the hedge-bottom, where I had made three or four comfortable nests, and I always collected the eggs as soon as possible, sometimes a dozen at a time. My mother never told me that we were doing anything wrong, but no one else knew that she didn't have to buy any eggs for several months.

When I was about 10 years old, Mr. Beck moved to the Poplars Farm, which had been in the occupation of Mr. Rogers, the General Secretary to Messrs Stanley Brothers combined brickworks and collieries. He went to South Africa to start up some brickyards there, and he took several of the best skilled workers with him, I was told in later years that the venture had been very successful.

**A.H. Rogers and G. Beck,
officials at Stanley Brothers, 1902**

I used to go to the farm very often, but eventually as Frank grew older, his interest in me quietly faded out, and in later years he went away to work. I have never seen him since, but I have often thought of him, we were good pals, and his influence did me a lot of good, just at the time when a boy is always ready to follow a good example.

Another friend of Frank's that I liked, he also attended the Bablake School, was Mr. C. H. Betts, who became a very popular School-master at several different Nuneaton Schools.

I made several other friends after this, one in particular, Jack Bloxham. His father looked after the Brick-yard Farm, where the horses were kept, about a dozen strong cart-horses. Most of the transport of materials was done by wagons and carts, motor lorries had not come into action then, 1895. Mr Bloxham Senior was a fairly tall man, sturdy and strong, he had a strong black beard, and they had a family of 21 children. His wages were about 30 shillings per week, but he had no rent to pay, a very big garden full of all kinds of fruit trees, and plenty of room for vegetables. He had free coal, a couple of cows, so they had plenty of milk and butter, pigs and fowl

29

which provide pork, bacon, ham, and plenty of eggs. These were all fed on the waste (and I guess, sometimes, not on the waste), and cost nothing to keep. These incidentals made up to some extent for his small wage.

One of the happy memories of my boyhood was when in the cold winter months, Jack and I would sit and talk in the harness room, where there was a small coal burning stove, which was always kept burning so that the harness and horse-rugs would dry. To be there, hearing the horses moving in their stalls, rattling their chains, and munching their oats and corn, was so peaceful and I have never forgotten it. Jack always brought several eggs every night, and boiled these on the stove and we had a good 'tuck-in'.

Another pal of ours was a lad named Tom Whetstone, a good quiet lad, and we had some good times together. Our house was directly opposite The Black Swan Inn, a comfortable old-fashioned building, low ceilings, red quarry floors, cozy and warm, and the beer was good. The public houses at that time were open from 6a.m. in the morning till 11p.m. at night, and all the cleaning etc., had to be done while the customers were in, unless the Landlord and his wife got up very early hours of the morning.

If any workmen on the day-shift, who was fond of the booze, felt a bit workshy, he would drop into the pub and have a day's drinking, if his credit was good. Some of the men on the night-shift would call in on their way home, and some of them would stop in their working clothes, dirty hands and faces, and most of them would go home rolling drunk at dinner time.

Most of the men had their drinks on the slate, i.e. the Landlord used to keep a 'slate' or book where he entered and kept account of all that the customer had, and they were expected to settle-up on pay day, so it all depended on the customers credit as to how much beer, etc., he was allowed to 'strap'.

On Saturdays, after mid-day, I used to get in our front window upstairs, and watch the 'fun' (?). Men used to come out of the pub, drunk or nearly so, and there would be sometimes two or three fights going on at the same time, stripped to the waist, they would fight for hours, knock each other silly, the blood was flying, and the language was vile.

There was only one village Constable, and he always found somewhere else to go while this was going on, (sensible man). When the battle was over, the men either rolled or were carried home, drunk, 'stoney broke', or nearly so, and the wives had to make do with what money they had left, and get what they could on the 'book' from the local tradesmen, who got their accounts settled sometimes, and if they were not careful, sometimes allowed too much credit, and put themselves either in the clutches of the wholesalers, who charged them an exorbitant price for their goods, or else they closed down, and went bankrupt.

Just at this time there was a 'bruiser' named J.H. who was the terror of all the publicans in the district, whenever he went into a pub they expected a row or trouble. One pub that he often went in, the publican was so frightened, that he always went out of the way, and left his wife to deal with him.

Eventually this publican left, and the place was taken over by an ex-Army Sergeant Major, 6 foot in height, and an ex-champion heavyweight boxer. This publican, we will call him Bill, had been told about J.H. and was standing at the pub entrance one day, when J. H. walked up to him. They both looked at each other, and J.H. said, "So you are the new Landlord, move over, I want to come in and have a pint." Bill replied, "So you are J.H., the terror of the publicans, well, you are not coming in here". J.H. squared up and said, "I'm coming in, you can't stop me." Bill just let him 'have one', and knocked J.H. about five or six yards onto his back, he didn't go there again.

Chapter 3

The 'Good Old Days', they were for some, but not many. Dad was a pretty heavy drinker, a good bass singer, but he spent most of his spare time in the pubs, he used The Black Swan quite a lot, this caused quite a lot of trouble between him and my mother. He was paid monthly, and he was usually broke and had spent all his pocket money after the first week, and Mother had to provide his drinking money for the rest of the month.

I always (and the rest of the family) dreaded weekends. He always played 'hell-up', and made Mother's and our lives miserable, and it wasn't until I tackled him later on in life that he altered his ways, and home life became much more comfortable and happy, and my mother had some peace.

He was a very competent Under-Manager, very strict, and never slacked or neglected his work, it was woe betide any man who was careless or idle, and may be risking not only his own safety, but others' as well. He got good results and could he cuss, usually when he made his first examination of the districts, nearly everyone had to go through the 'mill', he was much more reasonable on his second round. I know, I worked under his control for several years.

When he was appointed, sometime in the 1890s, the colliery, which was only a small one, was on its last legs. The output of coal very small, and the roads very bad, but he soon got things moving, and the output increased rapidly. Through his good practical management, No. 5 pit (Metz) made a big difference to the profits of the Griff Colliery Company Ltd:, and I heard it said that a good portion of the money that the company made out of Metz, help them to develop Griff No. 6 'Clara' Colliery, which at a later date, became one of the best collieries in Warwickshire.

Dad often had several colliery officials to see him on Sunday mornings, and they used to sit there reeling their yarns off, smoking and drinking beer (Dad always had a 9 gallon barrel of beer in the larder) until it was time for the pubs to open. Incidentally, Mother had to pay for the barrel of beer.

I sat in the background lots of times, ears cocked, and thoroughly enjoyed all the matters that they talked about, the tales they told, sometimes very funny, often crude, obscene, and some vile and filthy.

I heard Dad telling them once, that he had 'landed' thousands of tons of best quality coal into the trucks at 2/4 per ton[3], this covered all the costs of the wages, timber, steel girders, pit ponies, repairs to coal-tubs, etc., and included his magnificent salary of £2-2-0 per week, plus free house, coal, wood, oil, and two weeks holiday every year with pay.

---

[3]*The pre decimal system of United Kingdom currency was quirky to say the least: One Pound was made up of 20 Shillings (1/-), and each Shilling was worth 12 Pennies (12d). The two and a half shillings coin (2/6) was called a half-crown, recalling the historical 5-shilling crown coin, and the two shillings coin (historically a florin) was called two bob (one shilling was known as a 'bob' for reasons unknown). Below a shilling, a sixpence coin (6d) was 'a tanner', the three penny coin (3d) 'thruppence' or 'thrup'ny bit' (as it was octagonal). Below this come the 'coppers' (after their lovely bronze colouring): the two pence coin (2d) was 'tuppence' and 1d coin was a penny. A half-penny was shortened to 'a'p'ny (pronounced 'ape-knee), and quarter-penny was the beautifully named farthing (from the Anglo-Saxon feorthing, a fourthling or fourth part). George's weekly salary of £2-2-0 was Two Guineas: a Guinea being a rather aristocratic 21 shillings, used when trading horses and furniture: the original guinea was called the Sovereign, a gold coin minted between 1663 and 1813.*

One of his pals was a North Countryman named Jacob Roseby, who was the under-manager at Griff No.4 Colliery, and his Northumbrian brogue always interested me. He had a brother, Tom, working under him as a deputy, a roguish sort of man, always fond of a joke, a drink or two, and he liked the ladies, (more about him later).

It might interest readers of this book to know some of the prices of goods in the shops, public-houses etc. Best quality meat, beef, mutton, pork, etc., was plentiful and cost roundabout 6d per lb[4], the cheaper cuts were about 4d per lb, offals about the same price. Butter 10d to 11d per lb: Best English lard, 6d per lb, cheese, prime English 7d or 8d per lb:, New Zealand and American varieties, Danish as well, from 5d to 6d per lb. Eggs, new laid, 15 to 18 for 1/- (one shilling and no pence), Irish and foreign eggs, 20 or more for 1/-. Bacon, 4d, 5d, 6d per lb, top grade about 8d per lb. Sugar, 8 lbs for 1/-. Tea, Coffee and Cocoa very cheap and good quality.

Best mild beer was 3d per pint, a weaker type 2d per pint. The stronger brews of ale or beer could be obtained for 4d, 5d, or 6d per pint, Porter at 3d per pint, "Guinness" at 2d per half pint bottle, and best bottled beer at the same price. All kinds of tobacco were cheap, from 2d per oz[5] upwards, "Wild Woodbine" Cigarettes one penny per packet of five, so-called better grades a little dearer.

---

[4] *lb = one pound in weight, equivalent to 0.45 kilos.*
[5] *oz = one avoirdupois ounce, equivalent to 28.3 grams. If you struggled with British pre-decimal currency, let's see how you fare with the Imperial system of measuring weight. It was originally based on a grain of barley: 7,000 grains weighing one pound (each pound was split into 16 ounces of 437.5 grains, and each ounce divided into 16 drams, of 27.34375 grains each). There were 14 pounds in a stone, 28 pounds in a tod, 8 stones in a hundredweight, 26 stones in a sack, and twenty hundredweight in an old ton. There will be a test later.*

Brandy, 4/6 to 6/-, Whisky, all the best-known brands, 3/6, Rum, 2/6, Gin, 2/-, best quality Port and Sherry 1/- upwards, or per pint bottle. Tarragona Port 1/- per quart.

Coal, good quality, 6d per cwt.,[6] rents were very small. Clothing and household goods cheap and very good quality. All kinds of fruit and vegetables were cheap and plentiful, bread was about 2d per 2lb loaf (and it was bread, not dry "chaff" that they serve us with now) and a good many of the people made their own bread and cakes. Milk was 1½d per pint, and mineral waters 1d per large bottle.

This was in the Victorian Age, 1895, but to counter-balance these low prices, wages were very small, and working hours very long. There was a terrible lot of unemployment and short time working, and all Bank holidays meant a short week to follow. If a man fell ill and got injured there was no sick pay, and the doctor had to be paid (sometime) or he would not attend the case. More than 50% of the children belonging to the lower working classes were poorly clothed and the boots or shoes they were often worn and tumbling to bits.

What a contrast, when you look at the school-children of the present time, well-fed, clothed properly, and under the National Health Service, their physical well-being is much better.

Some of the boys, from the age of 10 years until they left school, worked half-time in the brickyards, or as errand boys for some of the shop-keepers, and the girls had to go into 'service' for the 'better class', and in return got their 'keep' and very little money.

One of my brothers was apprenticed to a local butcher and all he got was his board and lodgings for 1/- per

---

6 *Cwt = hundredweight, equivalent to 50.8 kilograms. Men delivering coal would heave these around all day long.*

week. Lads leaving school commenced working for a very small wage, the work was hard, and the hours long. Girls were much worse off, if they worked in factories they were kept up to their work like slaves, the hours were much too long, the factories cold and comfortless, and the toilet arrangements were sometimes very crude and poor, privacy was never considered by most of the factory owners.

The only alternative was to go out as a servant, and work hard for their 'keep', wages varied from 2/- upwards per week. 'GOOD OLD DAYS', and the Tories ruled the roost, and got their work done for a wage that was always based on a figure which was always a few shillings less than the amount needed to ensure a decent living, saving for the future was impossible. Holidays were out of the question for the majority.

Nuneaton Market Place, 1890s

The main industries in Nuneaton were coal mines, brickyards and quarries, and all the land round about the town was owned by the people who had big financial interests in these concerns.

When Coventry and Birmingham were getting dozens of manufacturers starting up the new and old factories a fair number tried to obtain sites for factories in Nuneaton. But their offers were turned down by the landowners, because they had the idea that the lighter, cleaner, and in many cases better paid work would attract the men, and cause a shortage of labour in the heavy industries.

Coventry expanded rapidly, while Nuneaton was at a standstill for many years, and a large proportion of the people had to work out of town. One instance, only, the Rugby B.T.H. Company[7] tried hard to obtain a suitable site, but all their offers were turned down, and they now employ thousands. Vested interests and Tory policy in the 'Good Old Days'.

My youngest brother, Sidney, was born in 1894, and soon after we had to leave our lovely house for one very close by in the same street, but we were not very settled there, and shortly afterwards moved to a large double-fronted house in Queen's Road, the name of the house was Appleton Villa. It is now a flourishing ironmongery and hardware shop. This was about the year 1896, and I was transferred from Heath End Mixed Church School to Shepperton Boys School, where I had a very happy time for the last 18 months of my schooldays

---

[7] *B.T.H.: British Thomson-Houston, subsidiary of General Electric in the U.S.*

**Chilvers Coton National School, 1900s
(now the Chilvers Coton Heritage Centre)**

The late Mr. G. H. Mosedale was the Headmaster, and Mr. Fred Mosedale was the next in command. They were both good sound men, real practical teachers, kept the boys up to their work without any bullying, and dealt with any unruliness firmly, but without harshness. 'Fred' was my teacher, I liked him.

**Mr. G.H. Mosedale, Headmaster, Chilvers Coton
National School, 1902**

Mr. George Mosedale did not have much to do with our class, but he must have noticed my work, as when I went to ask him for my Clearance Leaving Certificate, he remarked, "Well, George, my boy, I am sorry you are going, I thought we were going to make you a pupil teacher". He asked me what I was going to do, and I told him that I got a job as an errand-boy at Mr. Clare Speights, Photographer, Coton Road, Nuneaton. He patted me on the head and wished me good luck.

I made a start there on the Monday following my birthday, November 18, 1898. There was plenty to do, but the work was interesting, and the time passed quickly. The hours were 8 a.m. to 6 p.m. weekdays, Thursdays 8 a.m. to 1 p.m., and Saturdays I usually worked until 8 p.m. for which I received 1/- extra. My wages were 6/- per week, about 1½d per hour.

Mr. Speight was a very intelligent man, very particular, rather vain about his work, personal appearance, and the cleanliness of his shop and studio.

Clare Speight, 1902

He was also fussy about his food. When we were in the dark-room developing the negatives on Saturday nights, (Saturday was always a busy day, and it usually took about two hours to get all the developing done, that was when I earned my extra bob), Mr. Speight talked to me about a good many different subjects, but his favourite subject was Socialism. The I.L.P.[8] was just getting into its stride about this period, 1898, and he was one of the early members of this party, they held weekend meetings at convenient places all over Britain and usually cycled there, they were nearly all members of the Clarion Cycling Club.

At that time, the Clarion was about the only Labour newspaper in England. Robert Blatchford was the Editor, and A.P. Thompson was a regular contributor, G.B.Shaw also, and many others of the 'Old Brigade'. Most of it was for the love of the cause, the money was just not there.

Mr. Speight used to drill Socialism into me whenever there was any opportunity, especially where we were doing the developing in the darkroom. When he was retouching the negatives, (a very tedious job) I had to read the Clarion to him. Thus another Socialist was born, and the efforts of Mr. Speight improved my outlook on life, increased my intelligence, and no doubt has had a big influence on my life throughout the years. I stayed with him for about two years and then left to go into the engineering shop at Stanley's Brick Works.

---

[8] *International Labour Party*

Speight's Photographers, Coton Road, 1910s

Chapter 4

When we moved to Appleton Villa in 1896, Dad had been transferred to Griff No. 4 Colliery, Mr. Jacob Roseby had got into the 'bad books' of Mr. E. F. Melly, the General Manager, and he told Dad that if he would take over No. 4, Mr. Roseby could take over No. 5 'Metz', which was not such a large colliery as No. 4 Griff, and so keep his position as undermanager. Mr. Roseby carried on for a time, then resigned, and went to Haunchwood Colliery.

Mr. E.F. Melly, J.P., 1902

When he left, we moved from Nuneaton back to Chilvers Coton, into the Colliery House in Heath End Road, a lovely old house, roomy, plenty of large outbuildings, a very large garden, full of all sorts of fruit trees and bushes, and we also rented a lovely little paddock close to the house.

I think I have given you a good lot of information about Dad, so you will all know about what sort of man he was, it was a pity that he was so nasty tempered. He was a good worker, intelligent and very conscientious, not a good husband, he made my mother's life hell sometimes, admitted, he had cause, but Mother's good points counter-balanced her little failings a thousand times over.

Mother was a grand little woman, she was only about 5 feet in height, very vivacious and attractive, full of life and fun, courageous, a good manager, and she never seemed tired until later on in her life. I think that this was the real cause of the bust-ups, she was rather fond of some of the opposite sex, and I never blamed her, nor do I now, and I'm always glad to think that I stuck up for her through thick and thin, protected her from the results of his (Dad's) violent temper, and eventually tamed him. He did not realise her value to him, until he lost her. Mother was a good cook, and nothing was too much trouble for her, she would help anybody who was in trouble, nurse and sit up with anyone who was ill.

She was a very good mother, careful yet generous, saved the coppers and gave many a bob away to anybody who was down on their luck, all who could tell the tale. We were always good pals, and her last words to me before she passed on in 1922, were, "Look after your Dad, George, I know I can rely on you".

My eldest brother, Jack, was married and left home before I really knew him, he was a lot like Dad, quick, nasty temper, clever, but never looked ahead, he had some grand opportunities if he had only taken advantage of them, but such is life. He was employed as a Clerk in the Griff Colliery Offices for many years.

Ernest, another brother, was different in temperament altogether to Dad and Jack, very even tempered, quiet, good-natured, and generous when he had got any money. He was a good reliable workman, very conscientious, but he had a lot of bad luck, lots of ups and downs, though he eventually, towards the latter part of his life, had a comparatively comfortable period.

44

Florence (Flo, we called her,) was my eldest sister, and Mother's right hand for a number of years. She was a lot like Mother must have been in her younger days, though she lacked Mother's courage and fighting spirit to hold her own. Flo looked after us youngsters and worked like a steam engine helping Mother with the housework.

Later on, she married at Shropshire man named Noah Pitchford, I think he must have inherited some of his Jewish namesakes' carefulness for he was one of the most tightfisted men I have ever met, poor old Flo never knew what it was like to squander a bob or two, for the greater part of her married life. Mother used to play 'hell-up' about him, and told his name with knobs on, lots of times. Flo had a family of five children, reared them on very little money, and they all turned out to be a credit to her.

My brother Albert was three years older than me, he was a mixture of Dad and Mother, very hasty tempered, quick, clever, and determined to get on in life, independent, very careful in some ways, but often generous to an extreme point, and was often let down by many of his so-called friends many a time. He was made an apprentice to the butchery trade, when he left school at the age of 13 years his wage was one shilling per week, board and lodgings, and he had to work about 70 hours a week, (more about him later).

My sister May was the pet lamb of the family, she was three years younger than me. Very gentle, a bit vain, fond of flattery, and had just a trace of snobbery, she ought to have gone on the stage. As a matter of fact, she was a child actress up to the age of 12, and this made her more self-assured, and confident of her own abilities. Generous, peace loving, and energetic to a certain extent, she always looked much younger than her age.

45

Sid, my youngest brother, was also a pet lamb, perhaps because he was the youngest. He was a very clever chap with anything mechanical, and he became a good practical Electrical Engineer, though I'm sure the theoretical side of the business was a bit beyond him, he was too fond of outside interests, and did not bother to study the why's and where-fores. He was very generous, vain, good company, but not a very deep thinker, anyhow, he was the lucky one of the family, the girl he married was the only daughter of a Cinema Owner, and he was always well britched[9] from that time. I was the guardian of May and Sid, and they were always left in my charge when Mother and Dad went out at weekends and holiday times. That's the description of my family, my own character will be left for all who read this book to deduce, and think what I was like in my younger days, so now back to Appleton Villa.

---

[9] *Britches: a good old Midlands word for trousers.*

Chapter 5

Appleton Villa brings back to me many happy memories, it was a very large house, double-fronted, three large rooms, and a very big scullery on the ground floor, large hall and big larder. There were three very large bedrooms, and a good-sized bathroom, in which a single bed could be put up when required.

In Nuneaton at that time there was only the Theatre Royal to provide relaxation, no Cinemas or Music Hall, so it was a case of either the pubs or the theatre when anyone wanted a night out. Theatrical Companies usually stayed one week at a time in the town, though sometimes if it was a Repertory Company, or an Opera Company, they might stay two or three weeks, especially if the public response was good. Mother fixed up two of the rooms specially for the leading members of these Companies, and at a pinch she would let them have two bedrooms, and we, the family, had to make the best of circumstances for that week. This did not happen very often, only when the leading man and his wife perhaps had their daughter, or some special friend, whom they wanted to stay with them.

Some of the actors and actresses we had staying with us became quite famous in later years, though others faded out as the Cinema became popular. The Tearle's, Greets, Wilson Barrett, Dr. Walford Bodie, Harry Starr, Moore Marriott, Lawrence Irving, W. H. Gilbert, Veronica Brady, and dozens of others, who made good in musical comedy and film work later on.

My sister May had deputised for the child part in "East Lynne", and made quite a success of it. One of the Companies which came to the Theatre, was under the control and management of Mr James Bell and his wife who was the leading lady and starred as Miss Annie Bell, the name of the play was - the City Outcast.

The play was about a small child, who was the heir to a small fortune, and the efforts of the scoundrelly next of kin uncle, to get his child out of the way, so that he could claim the money. The child part was the 'plum' of the play and Mrs Bell persuaded Mother to let May go with them on tour and play this part, as the child who was then playing the part was getting too big and too old.

May Clarke

May was a very successful child actress and had some very flattering reports in 'Stage', and all the local papers of the towns and cities they visited. She was with Mr. and Mrs. Bell about three years, and they travelled all over England, Scotland, and parts of Wales. The 'Bells' would have adopted her, but Mother would not consent to this, and eventually May came home again.

I was an enthusiastic lover of the theatre, especially the better type of play, and when Miss Greet, the business manager for the Ben Greet Company, stayed at our house she often had a good talk to me, sounded me on my views of different plays, actors, actresses, and their capabilities, good and bad. She stayed at our house several times, and always wanted to know where George, the hyper-critical one, was, and what I was doing.

The bottleneck from Queens Road

At that time, about 1898, there was a public-house, the Crystal Palace, which was situated at the Queens Road entrance to the Market Place. It was quite a bottleneck just at this point, the main road was about nine foot wide, and the footpaths each side were only about three foot wide, in later years the building was demolished, and the licence transferred to a new public-house in Attleborough.

The licence in 1890 was held by a very enterprising businesswoman named Mrs. Wrighton, who in her younger days had been a cabaret singer and hotel manageress in South Africa. She ran the Crystal Palace on modern lines, (at that time) and had part of the pub converted into a large singing room, with the bar at one end, and a stage with room for piano, etc., at the other. She called it the Bohemian Club, and it became a very popular meeting place for all the 'sporting' business men, amateur singers, good and not so good, the actors and actresses from the theatre, some of the Don Juans on the prowl, and one or two good natured 'ladies' of leisure.

The bottleneck from the Market Place

When Mrs. Wrighton got to know about the proposed demolition order, she bought a large square plot of land, and two or three houses in Queens Road, which she converted into a large house at the front, lovely garden with rustic shelters and bowers covered all over with rambler roses and a large fountain in the centre. On a large part of the land there was a large wooden building with a brick built frontage into Victoria Street, there was room for several hundred people in the building, with a large bar and refreshment room at the back end. Mrs. Wrighton's intention was to run this on continental lines, have artists to sing and dance, run dances, and allow the customers to sit in the garden if they wished.

Smoke Room, Crystal Palace, 1900s

She laid out quite a small fortune, and then, to her astonishment and dismay, the Licensing Magistrates would not grant the Excise Licence, and thus prevented her from selling spirits, wines, and ale. This nearly ruined her financially, but she let the building to a body of men who formed a Working Men's Club, and also the house to a good tenant, and then went back to South Africa until the property was sold. The Club carried on for some time, and then owing to the poor management and other breaches of the law, was closed by the police authorities.

It was reopened as a Moving Picture Theatre as the cinemas were then termed, and in 1912, it was bought by Mr. S. Smith, of Bradford, who ran it successfully for a number of years, and in 1927, built the Palace Cinema in Queens Road, and went on to further success.

My brother Sid married his daughter, the only child, and when Mr. Smith died, Sid and his wife became the owners, and the Palace became very popular. Mr. Smith was a grand old man, quiet, gentle, very generous. He was a real Socialist, both in thought and action, many an old man missed him, he always gave them 2/6 if he thought they were hard-up, and during the Miners Strike in 1921, he helped lots of families, and also allowed the use of the cinema, free, for the Miners meetings.

Now, back again to 1897, I said I was very fond of the Theatre. I liked good plays, opera companies, and at that time we had some really good musical comedy companies which came to Nuneaton, The Belle of New York, The Quaker Girl, The Merry Widow, Floradora, The Arcadians, Our Miss Gibbs, The Broken Melody, and many more too numerous to mention. Sousa[10] came with his band, and played all his famous marches, what a conductor, his energy was remarkable, he was a human dynamo.

The admission fees that time were (no tax) Front Circle 2/6, Back Circle 1/6, Front Stalls 1/6 (close-up to the stage for the Don Juans to get a good view of the chorus girls and dancers), Pit Stalls 1/-, Back Stalls 8d, Gallery 4d. It was a good night's entertainment, and cheap.

---

[10] *John Sousa was a world famous America band leader*

The Hippodrome Theatre, Bond Gate, 1900s

Chapter 6

There were some 'rum' characters in Nuneaton at that time, R., the provision dealer, S., the auctioneer, these two used to go out on the booze, and when they got warmed up would argue and play 'hell-up', until they decided to leave, then R. would 'swipe' all the glasses off the table with his stick. Next day they would call and pay the Landlord all that he asked for, to cover the damage.

M.B., the chemist, who was the family adviser for many of the people, and he was known as the 'Ladies Friend' - why? I leave you to guess. W., the old-fashioned Grocer, his shop always looked like something out of Charles Dickens' antique shop window, full of large fancy tins of tea and coffee, the smell and aroma of spices and roasted coffee beans, and the old Grocer standing in the doorway, short white apron, velvet jacket, and a round smoking cap on his head. Then there was E.S., the tailor, who always played the leading part in all the Amateur Dramatic productions, he missed his vocation, I think that he would have made a great tragedian. There was one young lady, Miss A., who was very well developed in the right places, neither Marilyn Monroe nor Diana Dors could hold a candle to her, she got plenty of admiring glances, but didn't make a future out of it, like they have done.

There was a certain attractive young lady, who had been 'playing the game' with eight or nine of the sons of the well-to-do businessmen of the town, and the usual thing came to pass, someone was responsible, but which one? She blamed W., and he married her. On the night of the wedding, the bachelors had a real Stag party to celebrate their escape. The marriage turned out to be a great success and they were very happy in later life. I could go on for hours, but I think I had better get on with something else.

One of my friends at that time was a lad named Charlie T., we were great pals, and once when he was staying with his Uncle and Aunt in the Country, I went for tea one week-end. They lived at a small farm, which had a flour-mill worked by water-wheel, the mill-rollers were made out of huge pieces of stone, and the noise in the mill when the corn was being ground was terrific. Charlie's Uncle used to grind the corn for most of the nearby farmers.

I always remember that day, and what a tea we had, home-made wholemeal bread, homemade butter, jam, new laid eggs, fresh water-cress from the brook, and home-made cake to finish up. Plenty of apples, pears, and all kinds of fruit. Poor old Charlie, he developed consumption (it was hereditary), and he passed on at the age of 14. Since then, I have always had an awful dread of this disease, I saw him gradually fade away.

Dad enjoyed himself while he was living near the centre of the town, he had several boon companions, who, like him, could sing a good song and tell a good tale or two, and they were always welcomed to the Annual Dinners, Suppers, etc., of the different Societies, they had free tickets for the event, and also free drinks, in return for their services and entertainment. One of them, J.T., had to be taken home in a wheel-barrow lots of times, he was a Scotchman, and used to knock the whisky back, until he was helplessly drunk and unable to walk.

One of the outstanding characters of the town was J.A., who was always called 'Flashy Jack', he ran a small livery stable, had four splendid grey horses, and catered for weddings, outings in brakes, waggonettes, and cabs. He was always smartly (and loudly) dressed in a checked jacket, waistcoat and, leggings, and very highly polished boots.[11]

In 1898, we moved back again to Chilvers Coton, to the colliery house I mentioned before, and this was a very happy period in my life. I had commenced work at Mr. Speight's, and I always enjoyed my leisure time in the garden and field, and doing fretwork, I saved up enough to buy a small stand camera, with which I earned myself a few shillings extra pocket money. I kept rabbits, and also pigeons, four pigeons that I had were proper homing birds, I sold them three or four times, but they always came back.

Dad bought an old pony and trap for about a fiver, I used to take May and Sid for country rides, the pony would never do much running on the journey out, but when we turned back for home, he would liven up and come back like a steam engine.

One day, when it was my afternoon off from work, I asked Mother where Sid was and she said "in the field". I went to look for him and he had put the pony's bridle on with the long reins buckled onto it, and he had wound the long reins round his neck and waist, fallen off, and the pony was slowly dragging him round, and would have eventually choked him, he was blue in the face when I got to him and unwound the reins.

What grand week-ends we had there, the only person who upset the harmony was Dad, with his bad temper and the 'hell-up' that he caused, but we got used to it, ignored him, and forgot all about him when he went to the pub.

I always remember one weekend, we usually had a very big joint of beef for Sunday's dinner and supper, and

---

[11] *'Flashy Jack' Albrighton's forge was opposite The Crown Hotel on the corner of Back Street and Bond Gate. It is now a shop.*

there was always plenty left for Monday. He came home in a vile temper for his dinner on Monday, and Mother said something which made things worse, he picked up a large meat dish with the joint on and bashed it into the corner of the kitchen. Mother would not clean up the mess, nor would she allow any of the family to do so. It lay there for three days, and Dad had to clean it up himself.

Chapter 7

In October, 1899, the Boer War broke out, and lasted until 1902. Volunteers were asked for, and I can remember the posters all over the county with Kitchener's eyes looking at you from every position you were in, and the words, 'Your King and Country Needs You'. Kitchener's finger was pointing, and always at the person who was looking. A fine work of art, whoever designed and executed it.

Lord Kitchener's recruitment poster

The pay was about a 'bob' a day, and strange to say, they got the men and won the war. This was a big business war if there ever was one. The only people who got any benefit out of it were, Cecil Rhodes, Jameson's, Barnardo's, Joel's, the Jewish Financiers, Diamond Merchants, and the owners of the Gold Mines.

Queen Victoria died in 1901, and was succeeded by King Edward VII, who was a big friend of the Joels, and some of the wealthy Jewish Financiers. 'Tommy Atkins' and 'Good Bye, Dolly Grey', were the popular songs, Rudyard Kipling wrote a recruiting song. The Army Bands were on parade, playing their inspiring marches and roped the men in.

Soon after the War started, a large number of the English, Scotch, Welsh, and other white members of the population of Johannesburg, who were engaged in commercial undertakings, or held positions as managers and supervisors in the Diamond and Gold Mines, left the district and came down to Cape Town or returned to their respective home-lands while the war was being carried on.

Among those who came back to England was a man named Abel Crumpton, his wife and two children. His parents lived at Oldhill, Cradley Heath, in South Staffordshire, and he settled there for a time.

In his younger days, he had worked at Wykin Colliery, and Dad had taught him a lot about mine management. He lodged at our house for several years, went back to Oldhill to work, got married, and then went to South Africa, then on to Johannesburg.

He came over to our house to see Dad and Mother and stayed for a day or two, and I asked him to take me back with him when he was ready to return to Africa. He told me that owing to the unsettled conditions he could not take me with him, but that he was going back on his own to find some small farm near Cape Town, settle there for a time, and then send for his wife and children and his younger brother, Sam, to come out to him, and that if I was still in the same frame of mind, and my parents were willing to let me go, I could join them and go at the same time.

Some months after, Dad and Mother had a letter from him, saying that his wife, children and Sam were going to South Africa in January, 1901, and that if they liked to send me at the same time, he would look after me and take me to Johannesburg, when the war finished.

We all went on the midnight train from Birmingham, and of course, the tears were flowing when I said goodbye to my mother, she said "Don't go if you don't want to, it doesn't matter about the cost of your passage money being wasted." The total cost, railway fare, sea journey, and incidentals amounted to about £15, quite a large amount in those days.

Union Castle liner 'The Ghurka'

After a long tiring journey we arrived at Southampton, and landed on the Union Castle Liner, the 'Ghurka', she was a medium-sized liner, and was I proud when we had a good look round, and knew we were southward bound, I could understand how the Pilgrim Fathers felt when they went 'Westward Ho'. There was a very thick fog, which delayed the sailing time about eight hours, and then away we went, the liner's band playing, flags and handkerchiefs waving.

Sam and I were in the "Steerage", and Mrs. Crumpton and the children in the 2nd Class Saloon. The food was good and plenty of it, sleeping accommodation moderate, and toilet arrangements rather primitive. The stewards were good chaps and very helpful, I got on well with them.

The sleeping bunks were in sections, constructed of metal framework, with strong wire mesh netting on which the mattress and bed-clothes were laid. The number of bunks were ten in a row, room between every other two, so that you could make your bed and get in or out, the bunks were three in number vertically, so that in each section there was room for 30 persons.

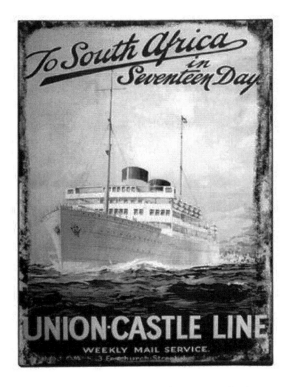

Advertisement for Union Castle Line

After the second night, I watched an old German, who was sleeping in a bunk close by mine, he was scratching himself for about an hour before he got into his bunk, very restless all the night, and when he got up very early in the morning, started scratching again. I waited until he went on deck, and then had a look at the bed on his bunk, and it was swarming with body lice. I called the Steward to have a look, and did he cuss, he didn't stop for a couple of minutes. He made a report to the Captain, the old man's clothes and the bedding were all burnt, and he was put in quarantine for the rest of the voyage.

The weather was cold and it was rather foggy, and the sea was rough, there was a lot of sea-sickness, which kept the stewards and deck-hands busy mopping up. When we were going through the Bay of Biscay, the waves were terrible, and tossed the big liner about like a cork, up and down, enough to break it into pieces. The weather was much better after passing through the Bay, and after one or two days we were into the sunshine. The sea was like a mill pond, and the air grand.

The first port of call was Las Palmas, to take in supplies of bananas, tomatoes, all kinds of fruit, and also to refill the coal-bunkers. It is a lovely island, the people are very friendly and easy-going, grand climate, all kinds of fruit and vegetables can be grown quite easily, and cost of living is very low. We went round part of the island, and then had two or three hours to look round, before leaving the port. The rest of the voyage was lovely, very hot, and the sea was as smooth as a mill-pond and I thought, this is the life.

One incident happened which kept Sam and I very much interested. We always sat at the stern of the ship late at night talking and listening to the rhythm of the propellers. The sick bay (hospital room) was next to where we sat, and there was a very young and attractive woman, the wife (?) of a very sporting looking type of man, made her assignments with numerous members of the passengers every night, the husband (?) kept watch, and they had bribed the sick bay steward to allow them the key and use of the room. It all eventually was found out, the steward got it hot and heavy from the captain, and was demoted.

When we were a few days from Cape Town, we passed the 'Kaiser Wilhelm der Grosse', and they signalled to our ship the news that Queen Victoria had passed on. Cape Town was in mourning when we got there, everywhere draped in crepe, and flags half-mast.

We went by train to Claremont, one of the suburbs of Cape Town, about 3 or 4 miles out of town, and after a light meal, Mrs. Crumpton, the two children, Sam and I set out for the farm, where we expected to join Mr. Crumpton. We reached the farm; it was only a small grape farm, the farm-house was a very poor looking place, dirty and neglected, and a man came out, asked us what we wanted, when we told him that we had come to live with Mr. Crumpton, he looked astounded and said "Didn't you know, he's been dead three weeks". He called Sam and I on one side, told us that some blacks had murdered him, and showed us the bloodstains on the walls of the living room.

We went back to Claremont, then to the Police Station, they confirmed the man's story, and said that all the money had been stolen, that there were no personal effects, and that the farm was only rented. We stayed at a small dirty hotel in Claremont a few days. Cape Town was full of refugees from upcountry, and there was no work about and prices were very high. Mrs. Crumpton and the two children then got fixed up by the Refugee's Welfare Committee, who found them accommodation and paid for her passage home later.

Sam had properly got the 'wind-up', I begged him to stop and try and get work, but he said "No, I am going home". All the money I had got when we landed was nearly done and I thought it was hopeless for me to stop on my own.

We went down to the docks in Cape Town, and the Union Castle Liner, the Durham Castle, was due to go back to Southampton the next day, we saw the Captain, and he told us that we could work our way back, as several of the Stewards had deserted, in order to join a Mounted Volunteer Division that was being formed, the pay was 5/- per day, while the regular Army pay was a bob a day.

We fetched our baggage straight away, and slept on board that night, the sea is not rough in the vicinity of Cape Town, but the waves swell up and down, and I was seasick for the only time going to Africa and back.

Poor Sam had to help the Stewards in the steerage, but I was lucky, I had to help the Stewards and the Cook in the 1st Class Saloon. One of my duties was to sweep the dining room, dust, and clean the brass-work; all the brushes, etc., were stored in a cubby hole in the fruit room, which was full of bananas, grapes, oranges, peaches, and all other kinds of fruit and nuts. The Chief Steward gave me the key when I wanted the brushes, etc., and usually said, "Now, George, don't bust yourself," but I had a good 'tuck in' every day. [12]

The Cook was an Italian, hot tempered and fiery, he was always grumbling about the work and his job. One day he said to me, "Ven I reach Sampton, you will see me viz ze girl on mine arm, big ceegar, plenty of money, ven ze money gone, ze girl gone, back to ze bloody ship, cook, cook, all ze day long, makes me seek, and drives me bloody mad." He was a good chap for all that, and taught me a lot about cooking.

We called at Madeira to get supplies, but none of the ship's crew were allowed to go on shore, so I didn't get the chance to have a wander round the island, but it looked lovely from the deck of the ship.

---

[12] *After the journey he vowed never to eat another banana again.*

When we reached Southampton, the staff of the ship made a collection for Sam and I, which covered expenses to get home, and a few shillings over. The Chief Steward begged me to stop and sign on as a member of the staff. I have often wished I had taken advantage of this offer, and sometimes wonder, "where would I be now ?" You never know what you are missing, and opportunity never knocks twice.

When I got back to Coton and home again, it was getting dark, Dad and Mother were out, and only May and Sid were in, so I had a big supper of bread and cheese, I had been longing for bread and cheese, as when on the liner, we always had hard biscuits and cheese. I was very tired and fed up, so I went to bed, and May told Mother when she came in, she came up to me, and we both cried tears of joy this time.

After a few days, I went to work in the Engineering and Fitting Shop at Stanley's Brickworks, and learned the rudiments of Black Smithing, and the manipulation of Drilling, Planing, and Milling machines. This lasted for about six months, and then Dad made the biggest mistake of his life, he resigned his position as under-manager at Griff No. 4 Colliery, to take over the tenancy of a public-house, The Turks Head, in Bilston, South Staffordshire.

Chapter 8

Bilston, at one time, had been a very busy and prosperous town, but in 1901, the rot had set in, and the Black Country went through a very bad spell for about 12 years, until the 1st World War started, when the trade boomed again for a period. Wages were terribly low, living conditions very poor, the Conservatives were in power, and didn't care how the working class people lived or fared, big profits and dividends were the only things they bothered about.

The Turk's Head, Bilston

There was one long street in Bilston, intersected by short side streets, courts and alleyways full of rotten tumbledown slum property. There were 39 public-houses in the street, and Dad and Mother must have been nuts when they were persuaded to take over the Turks Head. It was an old ramshackle place, draughty and cold, all quarry floors, which made a lot of heavy work, cleaning, etc., and business was very poor.

Dad had to go to work down one of the small pits, and I started work again at Sankey's, where they manufactured all sorts of copper, brass, and tin ware, which was sold all over Britain, and exported to all parts of the world. My wage was 6/- per week.

After about nine months of this, Dad got fed up, and left Bilston to go to Newdegate Colliery as a deputy, and told Mother to give the Brewery notice that we would be leaving the pub in a few months time. Meanwhile, I had left Sankey's, and started work for a building contractor, who was relining some blast-furnaces with fire-bricks, at Hindley's Iron Works, Netherton, near Dudley.

Bilston Railway Station

I got up at 5 a.m. in the morning, caught a train at Bilston at 5:45 a.m., travelled to Dudley, then walked nearly two miles to my work at Netherton. Wages 10/- per week and travelling expenses, for working and being away from home, from 5:30 a.m. until 6:30 p.m. My job

67

was to drive a small donkey engine, which worked a small lift inside the furnace, by means of a thin wire cable attached to the lift, which ran over a pulley wheel at the top of the furnace, down to the drum of the engine. The furnaces were about 30 yards in height, the workmen and all the material they used went up on the lift, so that I had to be careful, and not over-run the landing stage. The contractor was a short, very stout man, and one day, the men bet me a bob that I dare not let him come down with a bump, I lowered him down steadily half-way, then slipped the clutch out, and let him drop. When he had pulled himself together, he came to me, cussed a few minutes, and said, "You did that on purpose, you young so-and-so and so-and-so." I told him that the clutch had slipped. I won my bob.

Working for the Iron and Steel Company there was a labourer, a very strong, sturdily built hunch backed man, Bill was his name, he was wheeling and handling heavy pieces of pig-iron all day long, and he told me, "If you want to be strong and healthy, eat plenty of leeks every day, I live on them".

I passed what must have been one of the first water-cress farms on my way to work. The canal was passing along some high ground, and the farmer had constructed a series of pools in steps, about twelve in number, 6 foot by 20 yards wide, each section was well built and properly bricked, the water was diverted from the canal by means of a small ditch, to the top pool or bed, then the overflow ran from step to step and finally ran into a ditch at the bottom, then back into the canal when it reached the lower ground. The water-cress beds looked lovely, green and fresh.

While he was in Bilston, Dad made a pal of another publican, named Thomas Lindsey, he was a Durham man and had been under manager at Cannock Chase Colliery, for a number of years, he must have been nuts, as well as my parents, to take over the tenancy of a pub in Bilston. Besides that, he and his wife were both too fond of spirits, all kinds. She drank herself to death in a few months, and it only took another three years and he died from the same cause. The name of the pub that he kept was the Horse and Jockey, a more modern place than ours, and a little bit busier. It didn't pay, and Mr Lindsey only stayed there about 18 months. He had a large family of girls, and there wasn't much demand for female labour, so they had to do the serving and cleaning in the pub, and then idle the rest of the time away. The consequence was that two of them had to get married at very short notice, without much ceremony or money.

There was a young Scotchman called Jock who was after one of the girls, he was a member of the Bilston Police Force, a very nice chap to know when he was sober, but he was very fond of whisky, and did not know how to limit himself. One night when I called in to have a drink, Jock was drunk and raving mad, he was jumping over the tables, knocking the glasses over, and finally jumped over the counter to try and get hold of the girl, and police had to be called in. He was sacked from the Force, but he got another job, and married the girl.

There was a rather nice young girl named Janet Hickman, who came over from Cannock several times to visit the Lindseys. She was a pupil teacher, and we became very good friends, we had a lot in common to talk about, but I never saw her again after we left Bilston, I wonder where she is now ? There was another girl named Daisy Townsend, who was also a great friend of mine. The reason I mention her is because she was so much like my wife, dark, brown eyes, lively and vivacious, my own height, and we got on well together.

Old man Lindsey, after the death of his wife, hung round my Mother quite a lot, especially when Dad went back to Bedworth, to work at Newdegate Colliery, and left us to keep the pub open. Lindsey, was a clever man, he did his utmost to get me to like him, but I only put up with him for Mother's sake, he was one of those men who think they know it all, and he drank very heavily, whisky most of the time, which made him nasty tempered. Mr Lindsey and his family left their pub about the same time, and followed us to Bedworth, I think he had the intention to get work as a colliery official, but the drink had done its work, he had gone to 'seed', and his outlook was hopeless.

The Bilston United Football Club had their Headquarters and Dressing Room at our pub the year we were there. They won the Championship of the Birmingham and District League, and six Silver Cups as well. But what a mess they made, sludge and mud all over the place when they played their home matches, and the pub empty when they were away.

I usually went with them when they were playing away, Willenhall, where they made the most famous locks in the world, Walsall, the home of the Saddlery trade, Wolverhampton, cycles, hardware, and numerous other trades, Cannock, Pelsall and Hednesford, coal mines, brick-works, etc; Darlaston, Wednesbury, West Bromwich, nuts, bolts, screws, tubes, wire cables, anchors, pumps, and many more trades, Coleshill, Cradley Heath, Dudley, coal mines, brick-works, horse-shoes and nails, steel chains, all sizes, Kidderminster and Brierley Hill, coal mines, brickworks and carpet factories. These were some of the places where I saw them play. Bilston depended largely on the Steel-Works and Blast Furnaces, owned by Sir Alfred Hickman and Co. These works employed hundreds of men, and the wages were very good in the 1890s, but they were very poor when we were at the Turk's Head.

When Dad had found a house in Bedworth, he let the brewers know that we were leaving, they didn't make any arrangements for anyone to take over the tenancy, we sold all the ale, bottled beer, and Guinness, bottled all the wines and spirits ready to take away, and then when the removal van came, loaded all the bottles up with the furniture and other goods. The pub was then locked up, and Dad handed the keys to the Superintendent of the Police.

When we reached the Railway Station, the train was getting ready to start, we got into the compartment, Dad, Mother, May, Sid, and myself, then Dad leaned out of the window frame and shouted to his friend the Station-Master, "Bill, you can pull the bloody rails up when we're gone, we shan't want to come this way again".

Chapter 9

After looking round for work for several days, I started work at Newdegate Colliery as a trammer, (pushing the small coal trucks into the stall at the coal-face, and then pushing the full trucks back to the main road) and later on I was moved into the pit-bottom to help there.

While he lived at Bedworth, old man Lindsey became ill, and stayed at our home until he recovered. He had delirium tremens, or the 'blues' as we used to call them, he went on properly nuts for a time, and the things he did, also what he said, made as all rock with laughter. Poor old bugger, this was the beginning of the end.

After about eight months at Bedworth, Dad got a better position at Stanley's Colliery at Nuneaton, so off we went again, and old man Lindsey soon followed us. We lived in Grove Road, Stockingford, and old Lindsey and family lived in a house almost opposite on the other side of the road. I went to work at Stanley's Colliery. My first job was 'drawing' a small air engine, which pulled the full trucks up an incline, from a stall at the coal-face, the empty trucks ran down the incline, controlled by a brake on the drum of the engine, round which the wire cable coiled. The air which provided the driving power for the engine, and of course other engines, coal-cutting machines, pumps, and ventilation in some cases, was distributed all over the mine, through pipes from the Colliery surface, where some large compressors produced a pressure of about 80 pounds per square inch, which was maintained day and night.

Electricity and its uses was then only in its infancy, but stationary haulage motors were being installed in non-gaseous mines, and Stanley's was free from gas, so a number of these were placed where needed, and gradually replaced the air-engines, as they became old and worn-out, and the ways and means of the methods of using the powerful current became better known. I was moved from the small air engine to drive one of these motors, which was hauling the coal trucks from one of the busiest stalls in the mine.

Old Dick Hutt and his five sons were the stallmen, they were all big, strong, powerful men, and the men who worked for them had to be good workmen, or they couldn't keep pace with them. They were (the sons) all good Rugby football players, and three of them played for one of the famous Northern Union Teams.

After I had been driving this motor for about twelve months, I was moved to become assistant to a man named Bill Clarke, who was responsible for all the pipe-fitting to the coal-cutting machines, pumps, etc., he also had to do running repairs to the coal-cutting machines, which was all good practical experience for me. The only objection to this job was the amount of overtime Bill Clarke wanted me to work, they called him "Black Cat", because he was always at work. I have known him to be down the mine about 118 hours out of the 168 hours in a seven-day week. I worked some of the nights, but not the week-ends. When I grumbled when he wanted me to stop and work overtime, he always said "Now, George, my lad, the work won't kill you, and if you can only stand the time, the money will do you good". Poor old 'Black Cat', he worked hard all his life, and was a very clever fitter, and when he died he wasn't worth tuppence. Work hard, long, and prosper?

While I was working on this job, I was also on call as a spare motor-driver for all the motors in the mine, should anyone be ill or absent. Old Tom Roseby, the deputy, used to send for me and say "Now, Georgie, I want you to go to so-and-so motor today, and go there tomorrow, to see if the motor-driver turns up". He was a grand, jolly old chap. One day, when he came and sat down in the motor room, I said, "Tom, I have had enough shifting about, what about letting me go and work in one of the stalls, I would like to go in 'Hutts'. "So you are not satisfied, Georgie, what's the matter, you can stop on one regular motor if you like." "No, Tom, it's not that, you know I'm going to the Mining School, and I want more spare time, I don't mind working harder for more money and shorter hours, besides, I want to do a bit of courting like you, I know you like to turn 'em round. He looked at me and his eyes twinkled, then he smiled and said, "Georgie, my lad, you're not very big, even if you are strong and willing, your bones and muscles are not properly set yet, and I wouldn't let you go into Hutts' stall, they would work you to death".

A few weeks after this, I asked him again, he said, "Alright, you can go and work for so-and-so tomorrow". There was a smile on his face, he patted me on the back, and told me to see him the next day. The place where I went to work was halfway down the main haulage road, to tram the tubs from the stall, out onto the main haulage road, where a man clipped them on to the endless rope. Old Tom knew what he was doing. He meant to tame me: a grown-up man had been doing this job, and I was only just eighteen. Did I work, I had emptied my water-bottle by nine o'clock, and no chance of getting any more until 3:30 p.m. I was that tired and thirsty, I could hardly walk to the pit-bottom, and when I got home, I nearly 'busted' myself with tea and water. Next morning, I went to see the roguish old joker, and he looked at me, smiled, and said, "Well, Georgie, do you want to go there again?" "No, thank you, Tom, put me back with "Black Cat", I'll wait another year or so, and be ruled by you".

After some months, I was moved again to look after two or three pumps, which were in my Dad's district or section of the mine. This was the time when I saw the best side of my Dad's character. The way in which he

74

controlled his workmen, looked after their safety, and at the same time maintained a good regular output of coal from his district by method and good management, taught me some lessons that stood me in good stead in my later life. While I was working under him, I went into one of the stalls as a loader or filler of the coal tubs, then became a getter or pick-man, and eventually became a stallman or contractor when I had just reached the age of twenty. Dad always kept his eyes on me when he came into the stall, and told me my name with knobs on if I took any undue risks, or was careless in any way. Later on, I acted as shot-firer for the district when the permanent man was absent, and also acted as spare deputy when Dad was absent through illness or other reasons. This did me a lot of good, as I was never afraid to tackle any job.

I must now go back a year or two, as some things happened at that time which caused me more trouble at home. When we went to live in Grove Road, old man Lindsey had still got about two or three hundred pounds left, so he opened up a Butchers shop in the front room of his house, and my brother Albert managed it for him. They did very well for some months, and then the old man was taken ill again, and died in a few days.

Albert hadn't got any capital to carry on the business, so it closed down, and my brother went to work for the Co-Operative Butchery Department. Life was very uncomfortable at home before old man Lindsey died, he was a downright nuisance, always took over our house, especially at night-time, gorging and drinking whisky, brandy, ale, etc. Dad used to play 'hell-up' when he had gone home, and I had to protect Mother, lots of times, from getting knocked about.

One night in particular sticks out in my memory. I landed in home about 10 p.m. and Lindsey sat at the table feeding his face, it was a lovely dish of stewed beef, and

Mother asked me to have some. I refused to have any, and told the old man that it was time he had gone. He said, "What the hell is it to do with you, it's none of your bloody business to tell me what to do". My reply was; "It is my business, and if I had been in my Dad's place, you would have been out neck and crop long ago, you have caused nothing but a hell of a lot of trouble and misery ever since we knew you, bugger off to your own home." He did a bit of blustering and then went home.

Shortly after this, our house was wanted for the landlord's daughter, so off we moved again, this time to Toler Road, Nuneaton, this was in 1903.

Chapter 10

While we lived in Toler Road, life went along more smoothly and peaceably, Mother had had her lesson, and settled down, and Dad was much quieter. They still had a row now and again, but I always managed to calm him down.

I was now eighteen years of age, strong and sturdy, not a bad looking chap, either, although I say it myself. Next door to us there lived a married couple, he was in his 40s, and his wife was about 28, very gay, plump, and attractive. Her name was Nell, and I noticed that whenever I went up the garden, out came Nell, and she was always giving me the 'glad eye'.

One day when I got home from the pit, Mother was out, and had left my dinner in the oven to keep warm, so I stripped out to the waist and was washing myself, when I heard somebody behind me. I looked round, and Nell was there, she said, "I've come to wash your back, your Mother is out, you don't mind, do you?" Did I mind?, I ask you?, she washed my back, gave me a brisk rub with a towel, then caught hold of me, hugged me tightly, and made a rare fuss of me. Before she went away, I had promised to call in and talk to her when her husband was out, the signal, the front door ajar. This affair lasted for about six months, until we got our skates on again, and moved to a better house in Stanley Road. It was a very good house, with a nice garden, and life went fairly smoothly in the two years that we lived there, except for one or two minor rows.

I had been studying the technical side of mining for the previous two years, and attended the local coal-mining class held at the Lecture Room on Coton Road, the classes were held one night per week, Saturday afternoons and nights. After the first session, I got into the swing of it, and the next year, also the following two years, came out at the top of the list in the County Council Examinations.

These successes did not cut any ice with the colliery management; at that time, unless you were some relation of the owners, or of the management, or an articled pupil, students had to paddle their own canoe, no financial help, no time off to attend classes, and very little encouragement in any shape or form, not even a pat on the back. Class distinction was in force, all the best paid positions were held by relations of the coal-owners and the big shareholders, while men with much more knowledge and ability had to be content with the lower paid positions, and work like hell to keep them. This was in 1903.

What a difference now, under Nationalisation, any young lad or man who is willing to study in order to be able to become a good colliery official can rely on plenty of help and encouragement, time off for (paid) classes, and financial assistance when they attend Universities, in order to qualify for the Under-Manager's and Manager's Certificates, and higher degrees also. Wages were very low, hours long, and men and boys had to work very hard for a few shillings per day. Stallmen averaged about seven shillings and upwards, getters about 5/8, and loaders 4/8 up to 5/2, boys were paid about 2/- per day which was increased by a few coppers every birthday.

The price paid to the stallmen for getting the coal and landing it to the gate road varied from 1/7 to 1/10 per ton, according to the nature of the coal-seam, and the stallmen made their men work like slaves, in order to get a few shillings extra. The Miners Unions were not very strong then, and the Coal-Owners did what they liked with the men. There were stoppages at times for more wages and better conditions, but the Owners always had their way, and the men went back to work no better off, and perhaps, worse off than they were before. There were always about 20 or 30 men waiting every day for the undermanager to come to his office, so miners had to be good to keep their jobs.

The Motor Car Industry was just beginning to develop, and the Cycle Factories were very busy, lots of the young men were turning down the idea of heavy work in the Mines, Quarries, Brick-Works, etc., and going to work in the factories instead.

Wages paid to Railwaymen (all grades), Postmen and Post Office Staff, Town Council Employees, and also Office Clerks and Teachers were very low. The only thing that made life worth living was the low cost of living, and the luxuries of life, such as entertainments, tobacco and cigarettes, sweets, ales, wines, and spirits, were easy to obtain, and prices low. Although working hours were long, and wages were so poor, people seemed to be much happier and more contented than they are today, they didn't reach for the moon so much, and the pace was not so fast and more even.

After about two years in Stanley Road, my brother Albert wanted to start up in business again, as a butcher, in a new shop at Arbury Road, Stockingford, so off we went again to live at the rear of the shop.

Chapter 11

Albert had a tough struggle the first two or three years, but he worked very hard, and his overhead expenses were low. Mother helped him in the shop and in the preparation of the made up goods, pork-pies, faggots, sausages, etc., and I delivered the orders for him whenever I had the time. Eventually he built up a flourishing business, and made a good deal of money in later years.

Albert Clarke in the doorway of his butcher's shop on Arbury Road

Soon after he'd started, work fell off in the summertime, and many of his customers were on short time. I noticed him one week-end, looking very downcast and worried. I asked him the reason, and he said that a lot of his customers could not manage to pay their weekly accounts, and that he didn't know how he was going to find the cash for his week's supplies. I told him that I had got £50 upstairs, and that he could use that if he liked. This eased the situation for him, and he never forgot it, he helped me several times when I was up against it.

While we were getting settled in, and used to the routine, Mother worked very hard, Albert was sometimes very awkward and nasty tempered. Dad also started to play his old games again, creating hell-up, and making things uncomfortable for poor old Mother. It was a case of keeping the pair of them in check, but I did it, and the time came when I only had to walk in, and they shut up straightaway. I told Dad once or twice that if he didn't alter, I would take him outside and give him a damn good hiding, and both him, and Albert, knew that I could do it. That tamed them both, and Mother had more peace.

My main hobby at that time, apart from photography, was cycling. When the weather was good I went all round the district on my own, and usually called at a country pub for a pint of ale, and bread and cheese, half of a cottage loaf, and a quarter pound of good cheese for 3d or 4d, the cheese alone would cost you a bob nowadays. The company was always interesting in these country pubs.

My brother Ernest had gone back to his birthplace, Walsgrave, to live, he had a job as a winding-engineman, and he was more comfortable than he had been for some years. I went over to see him, and we went to a small village called Barnacle, where some of his wife's relations lived. They had a daughter named Alice, a bonny looking girl, who gave me the 'glad-eye' before we had been there many minutes. We went for a walk round the fields, and arranged to see each other again, the going was good while it lasted, but I thought it best to pack up after two or three months, I could see myself getting married by the time I was twenty, and a handful of children in five or six years, so I said good-bye to Alice. She married later on, and <u>had</u> a large family.

When I reached the age of twenty, I started going to the Drill Hall[13] on Saturday nights, where dancing was in full swing from 7 p.m. until 11 p.m. for the price of 6d, it was a good night's entertainment.

About this time, when in the town, I often noticed a couple of girls were always together, both small, and dressed very nicely, one had auburn hair, and the other had dark brown hair and eyes. I thought what nice girls they are, and I was very much struck by the brunette, it was love at first sight. I saw them lots of times, but as I was a shy sort of chap, I didn't get on speaking terms, just a smile from me and one in return from them.

One night at the Drill Hall, I had several dances with the auburn haired one, Esther, but my Little Lady had a boyfriend, who stuck to her like grim death all the time, so there wasn't any opportunity to talk to her. This went on for several weeks, and I danced with Esther, but the boy friend still held the fort. One Saturday night they came in, and the friend was not with them, but Esther had got a partner, so I gave her the wink, and she left me with my Little Lady, and we were soon good friends.

I asked her where the boyfriend was, she told me that they had had a "tiff", and that she was glad it was all over. I stuck to her all night, and when Esther saw how happy we were, she slipped off with her friend, so that I had to take Gertie home. Before I left her, I asked whether I could see her again on the Sunday night, and she said, "Yes, you can call for me if you like".

It was raining like hell on the Sunday night, but I went through it and arrived at the house, when I knocked on

---

[13] *The old Drill Hall was in Mill Walk, formerly a malthouse. It was completely destroyed in the 1941 air raid.*

the door, and asked for Miss Brooks, one of the younger brothers fetched Esther, who asked me in, and said that Gertie had gone to church with a friend. I thought, this is a poor start, but I started to talk to Esther, and hung on until Gertie came in. This was the beginning of a romance which lasted fifty years, and the longer we lived together, the stronger the bond became, we were always lovers and good pals, understanding and tolerant[14].

There was a rope-runner or bond-minder named Albert Gray, whom I knew very well at work, and one Saturday, when I went to call for Gertie, he was there talking to her mother. He looked at me and said; "So you are the one that's after our Gert, I am very pleased; you needn't worry, Liza, he's a real good chap, he will work, and look after her." He was Gertie's uncle, and her mother's youngest brother.

Mrs. Brooks was a grand woman, and as the years went by I became very fond of her. She was rather easygoing, very patient and tolerant, although there was a large family to provide for on very little money, she was always pleasant and good-tempered. Our "old Liza" deserved a medal if anyone did.

Mr. Brooks was a clever musician, and could repair and tune all kinds of musical instruments, he was also an agent for the sale of new ones, his main sales were pianos. He also played the piano at a pub over the weekends. Sometimes he had good weeks, but at other times, Liza had to do some scheming to make ends meet, especially while the children were young, but he never grumbled or complained, kept struggling on. [15]

---

[14] *Gertie at this time was a winder at Lister's Silk Factory.*
[15] *There is a family story that Liza would say "Levi, I don't know what we're going to have for tea today." And off he would go with his hand cart to move furniture or tune a piano, and come back with a bit of money for her to buy food. Levi was the only one in the family who had an egg for breakfast on Sunday, and*

During the time I was courting my Little Lady, whenever I called she was usually hard at work helping her mother, or looking out for the young 'uns. She was her mother's right hand, but it didn't matter how busy she was, or what she was doing, there was always a smile for me when I called for her, and I knew I had found the right one.

To any young man who wants to have a happy married life, this is the best advice I can give him. Go to your girl's home and notice how she helps her mother, looks after the children (if any), and the comfort of anyone there, if she is happy when doing this, she will make a good wife and partner. The same practice applies to a boy, with some modifications, go to his home, notice how he regards his mother, a good son usually makes a good husband, I don't mean a mother's 'pet lamb', but one who is willing to help and protect her.

The first time that I took Gertie home was several weeks after I had been to their house. It was my twenty first birthday and we held a small party to celebrate it, so she came and brought Esther as well. We all had a good time, and Mother told me that she thought I had got a very nice girl. My sister May was very pleased, as she had often got on my track, about mixing up with some rather well-known girls who roamed the town.

From then on, I didn't want anybody else, we were very good pals, and understood one another, always happy when we were together, and if money was short, we made the best of it, went for walks, and enjoyed ourselves talking, and planning for the future.

Esther had several different beaus, but eventually got going strongly with a butcher, named Alfred Daulman, and we all went out together lots of times, though I think

---

all the others had bread or toast, and milk. One Sunday, Sidney was told off for asking "I wonder what eggs taste like?"

84

we were much happier, when we went anywhere on our own, we were always contented and happy with each other's company.

The Family of Gertrude Brooks, 1905[16]

Back row: Eliza/Lizzie (1894-1983), Gertrude (1888-1955), Esther (1887-1925), Levi (1889-?), Fred (1895-?).

Adults: Levi Brooks (1862-1926), Eliza Brooks (1863-1950)

Front row: Sidney (1899-?), Mabel (1901-1959), Percy (1904-1970), Charlotte (1898-?)

---

[16] *Levi was born in Donisthorpe, Leicestershire and Eliza in Coalville nearby. They married in 1886, and Levi worked up from miner (1881), tile maker (1886), insurance agent (1901) to pianoforte tuner (1904). On George and Gertie's wedding certificate in 1909 his profession is musician: it is said he could play any musical instrument. His party trick was that he could spell any word, a challenge frequently laid down in the bar at the King William. In later years he ran the piano shop on Abbey Street (later Taylor's Music), and the family lived above it. Eliza, despite five miscarriages, gave birth to thirteen children, although four (twins Decima and Dulcie b1890, Frank b.1891, and Thomas b.1892, died in an 1893 outbreak of diphtheria. At one time 13 used to sit down to dinner, and Percy as the youngest had to sit at the sewing machine. Lizzie (back row left) made all the clothes worn in this photograph, except for Levi's suit and tie.*

Chapter 12

About this time, 1906, three men, who were very famous and well-known characters in later life, were just beginning to get into the public eye, though they were all different in their views and ideals of life. Keir Hardie was the first Labour man to become a Member of Parliament, Lloyd George was a very eloquent and far-seeing member of the Liberal Party. Winston Churchill, always the typical showman, had glorified his spectacular escape from the Boers in the South African War when he was a War correspondent, and then went on to Egypt to conquer the Sudan, and later, kept his name on the news with his many coloured hats of all shapes and sizes, one of which the Daily Mail did its best to make it a popular choice, the 'John Bull', a low crowned top hat with very curly brims, but the effort failed.

Winston became a member of the Liberal Party, and the main policy of the Liberals was Free Trade. The Germans, Japanese, and United States (to a certain extent) were flooding our markets and our shops with enormous quantities of goods, and undercutting our manufacturers in the world market, and even in Britain as well. Their goods were allowed to enter the country without any import duty (except in certain cases) being paid, while our exports to these countries had heavy tariff charges to overcome, with the result that we were unable to sell our goods abroad.

There was a very vigorous and active member of the Conservative Party, Joseph Chamberlain, a very prosperous Birmingham businessman, who made it his life's work to advocate the policy of Tariff Reform and preferential treatment for the British Empire. This was well backed up by the Daily Express, which was then in its infancy, Lord Beaverbrook had just taken it over after making a fortune in Canada. He has been a 'live wire' all his life.

The shops were full of all sorts of goods, food was plentiful, quality first class, and prices very low, but wages were very low, there was a lot of unemployment and short time working, and a large proportion of the population were poorly fed, clothed, and housed, while the upper classes, as usual, were living in the lap of luxury, and didn't care a damn. The German Empire, with the Kaiser Wilhelm and the powerful Army autocratic Leaders were building up a powerful fighting force and the naval strength was being increased slowly, and a lot of it secretly.

Our Army was still a voluntary one, the pay 1/- per day. The British Navy was still a strong and powerful fighting force, and the theme song was still, 'Britannia rules the waves', but the next line was all wrong, Britons were slaves, under the harsh economic conditions which were prevalent in these times, and from which there was no escape.

Chapter 13

I was a filler or loader down the mine at this time, and I thought, this sort of job is no good to me, I must step up a bit. The chief stallman was an old man named Charley Goodman, and he had his three sons working as fellow stallmen, along with another old man, 'Cordy' Townsend. One of the sons, Bill, who was usually called 'Nobby', was always a good pal of mine. I knew he was always hard-up after the week-end and that he was very fond of a pint or two.

So I said, "Nobby, get the old man to let me be a getter", he replied, "You are not old enough, George, wait till you get a bit older." But I stuck to him, and he said "what's it worth?", I promised 10/-, and he told me to bring it the next day, and I went with old Charley Goodman ('Fizzer') the next day to learn how to be a getter, but Nobby fetched me back to help him when he wanted any assistance, and I had to put up with 4d a day rise, instead of 8d a day which getters got more than loaders. Good old Nobby, he was as strong as a bull, and he showed me how to work, and made a good getter of me. He was always full of life and fun, and although he made me work very hard, I loved to be with him. He joined up in the 1914-1918 War, as a sapper in the miners section, and I never saw him again.

Old Cordy Townsend (so-called because he always wore corduroy trousers) was a jolly old character, very straightforward and a good conscientious workman. He liked his beer and always had plenty, but didn't let it interfere with his work, like some of the miners did, lots of them, if they had got a few shillings left over the week-end, always had the Monday off to have a booze-up and 'blue' the lot in.

The stallmen, at that time always took the blasting powder tin home with them (later on the Coal-Owners were compelled to provide a safe storage for them) and Cordy was on the afternoon shift one cold winter's day. It was snowing very hard when he and his mate were going home, and they called at their usual pub for a pint or two, there was a big roaring fire in the old-fashioned fireplace, and all the customers were clustered round it. They wouldn't move to allow Cordy and mate to have a warm, so Cordy said, "Watch me", threw the powder can on the fire, (he knew it was empty), and the men ran in all directions. Cordy picked the best seat, then told his mate to sit down, and laughed like hell as the men came in again.

The bona-fide traveller's bye-law was in force at that time: anyone who could prove that he had travelled three miles or more could claim to be served with alcoholic drinks on Sundays before the legal opening time. Several of the pubs in the outside villages round about Nuneaton always did a roaring trade on Sunday mornings, full of "bona-fide" travellers, and Cordy was always at one or the other.

Old Fizzer Goodman was a good old collier, but he was getting old and grumpy. When I was working with him, I used to do all the donkey work, get two or three stints cleared and straightened up, and think to myself, now I can do a nice bit of 'holing' or under-cutting the fire-clay or dirt from under the coal-seam, so that it made it easy to get, or to be blasted down with explosives, but old Fizzer would say, "Right ho, Georgie, move on, and get another stint or two ready". Still it was all in the day's work, and did me good later on.

During this time, I was attending the Mining School, studying at home, courting my Little Lady, and helping my brother Albert, the butcher, as much as I could in my spare time. Wednesday night, Saturday night, Sunday afternoons and nights were my usual courting times, but the weeks when I was on the nightshift cut out the Sunday night and midweek arrangements, unless the pit happened to be 'off', owing to slack trade which very often occurred during the summer months.

The Coal-Owners and the Management hadn't got the least bit of thought or consideration for the miners during these months. The men would get up very early in the morning, put their dirty pit togs on and walk through all sorts of weather, perhaps for a mile or two, and when they got on the pit-bank, the hooter would sound for a minute or so, which meant that there wasn't any work that day. So off they trudged home again, and not a penny for all their trouble, it was worth the dollar to put your dirty pit-togs on, but you got sweet bugger all.

As the Union got stronger, the Coal-Owners got a bit more considerate, and sounded the hooters at the different collieries the night before a certain fixed time when the pit was to be 'off' the next day, and men could either have an extra hour or two in bed, or get on with some spare time work. Owing to the large floating pool of unemployed people, conditions and wages were very poor in the factories, especially for female labour. They had no Unions, and no one to stick up for them and insist that better terms were needed. Girls worked from 6 a.m. to 6 p.m. for miserable pittances, and under the most primitive hygienic conditions. If they had the courage to stand up for their rights all they got was the sack.

These were the conditions in 1906, and several years later, and did not change until the Trade Union Movement got stronger, and then the first World War was looming on the horizon. The benefits of Tory Government and private enterprise, I ask you?, compare them with conditions and wages at the present time, and ask yourself what has brought about this revolution?, there is only one answer, <u>The Labour Party</u>.

Even at that early period, I was always having some debates at snap time. My views then were that coal mines, gas and electric companies ought to be Nationalised, so that the nation could control these industries, pay better wages, and make working conditions better for the men employed in these industries, and also that the Gas Works and Electric Generating Stations ought to be built as near to the collieries as possible, to save long-distance transport of coal, also, that every town and city ought to have its own coal distributing organisation. My contention was that if they could collect the ashes, they could also deliver the coal. How I do drag in my Socialistic theories, I can't help it, I had instilled into me when I was at the right age to remember them.

I was doing fairly well at work at this time, Charley Goodman's sons had left their jobs as stallmen, so I went in with Fizzer and Cordy as a stallman, along with another man named Jack Sandelance, and we worked well together. Old Fizzer was getting on a bit in years, and he had always been a bit of 'driver', so I used to pull his leg a bit, and tell him to liven up and get on with his work, when he was slacking and having a rest. He said to me once, "Georgie, you're getting married in a month or two, well, wait till you've been married a year or two, it'll take the old buck out of you." Old Cordy enjoyed it, and always told me to go and pull Fizzer's leg and get his hair off.

We all had to work hard in order to get a bob or two more than day wage, and often worked a good lot of overtime for nothing, a few shillings extra made a big difference in your outlook on life in those days, you could have a good night's enjoyment with a bob or two.

Jack Sandelance was a big chap, a good sound safe workman, rather slow, but sure. He was a North Staffordshire man, and he brought his brother-in-law to work for us, his name was Amos Jones, he was a good workman, very practical and farseeing, and we became good pals. He was about my age, and we kept up our friendship for a number of years, working together as stallmen, and enjoying a night out together, he would always follow me wherever I went to work; when I went to work as a Deputy at Denaby Main Colliery, he came to work for me, but it was too hot, so he went back to Nuneaton.

Later on, when I was at Swinton Common Colliery, I sent for him and found him a really good job. After World War No. 1, he wanted me to join up with him, buy a lorry, and start in the Transport business, but I had other plans, so we didn't get the lorry. I have realised many a time since that we missed a good opportunity, we might have had a good transport business now. His judgement was good.

Just at this time, 1907, I sat for the advanced Mining School Examination, and passed it easily, top of the list, gaining first prize with honours. Incidentally, the prize (a set of mining books) were presented to me by Sir John Cadman, who was at that time head of the Mining Engineering Department of Birmingham University, a position from which he resigned later on to become chief technical adviser to one of the big oil companies, which is now one of the largest in the world.

The same year I sat for a scholarship examination for Birmingham University, but came second, I could have gone in for it again the next year. Why I didn't, I don't know, because I'm sure I should have been successful, and probably this would have made a big alteration to my life.

Chapter 14

In the Summer of 1907, we had a nice holiday at the Isle of Man. There was quite a party of us, Mother and my sister May, Esther and Alf, and we all had a good time. Lawrence Irving was following in his father's footsteps at the Theatre in 'The Bells', and Hetty King at the Music Hall, famous bands were playing in the 'Dells', and the scenery, sea, and the sands were grand. One day, we went in a rowing boat, and I asked the old man who was rowing to let me have a go, I noticed him laughing at me after about ten minutes, so I said, "What's the joke?", he replied, "Look at the shore, I had better take over, or we'll soon be out in the Atlantic". Was my face red? We never forgot that holiday, we were so happy together.

I was courting my Little Lady nearly four years before we were married, and during that time had a number of enjoyable outings, not very expensive ones, the funds wouldn't run to it. Day trips most of them, to Leamington, Coventry, Birmingham, Leicester, London, Matlock, and many other places. Once we went to Coalville, Gertie's birthplace, to visit her grandfather.

He was a miner, and a grand old chap, very jolly, roguish, and full of fun. His advice when we were leaving was, "When you get married, don't pull opposite ways, or you will never get anywhere, both of you pull together, and you will overcome any trouble or trials that come along". This was good advice, and we did pull together most of the time, though sometimes I pulled a bit too much, when I got the urge to change my jobs, and Gertie had to come with me, sometimes against her better judgement and intuition, but she never grumbled, just settled down and made the best of it.

It is about time that I feel I ought to write a few words about Gertie's sister, Esther, who did her best for me in the beginning of my courtship. In fact, I think she thought I was making tracks for her at first, but all I wanted was to get in touch with my Little Lady.

Esther was a gay, good-natured, generous girl, not very tall, and had copper coloured hair. She was a good pianist, rather vain, but very good company. Domestic work was not in her line, though she would stick at dress-making for hours, which came in very useful and helpful to her mother, sewing for her and the family.

**Esther Brooks (left) with daughter Mabel
and mother Eliza, early 1900s**

She had not the same stability of character that Gertie possessed, but nonetheless, she was a really good sort of girl, I always liked her. She was married to Alf Daulman two years before our marriage, and they were fairly happy until later on in life, when being in business, and the 1914 to 1918 war, upset everybody's plans.

One incident I remember about Esther, was one Saturday night, I had attended the Annual Stallman's Dinner, and had too many mixed drinks, coupled up with one of two strong cigars, but I got properly drunk, how I landed up at Gertie's home, I don't really know. When I got there, I was absolutely helplessly drunk and sick as well. Gertie was amazed and wouldn't take any notice of me, but Esther took charge, went outside with me until I had recovered a bit, and then helped her mother put me to bed. When I woke up the next morning, I didn't know where I was, and I felt properly ashamed. When they told what had happened, I went home feeling <u>very small</u>. That was the only time in my life that I ever got helplessly drunk, but I've had some really good times without getting over the 'mark'. In fact, I think it is good, sometimes, to have a good 'bust up', it makes you forget your troubles, and acts like a safety valve.

Shortly after, Mr. and Mrs. Brooks moved into a house and shop in Queens Road,[17] in which he acted as an agent for a firm of pianoforte manufacturers, and also sold all kinds of musical instruments, at the same time he also went out cleaning and repairing pianos.

Gramophones were just becoming popular, and coming onto the market, but Mr. Brooks had got the idea that the sale of these would spoil the demand for pianos, so he would not try to sell them, nor records, and thus missed what would have been a profitable sideline.

---

[17] *72, Queen's Road, on the corner of Edward Street, now demolished.*

In 1908, Esther and Alf were married, and on Boxing Day of the following year, 1909, my Little Lady and I were married at the same Church, Chilvers Coton Parish Church, known all over the world by readers of the novels written by George Eliot as Shepperton Church, a lovely old building in a beautiful setting.

When I told Mother that I was going to get married, she said she was pleased, and that I had picked a really good sort of a girl, who she liked very much, and we ought to be very happy. Dad was a bit different when I told him. He looked at me and said "What's the hurry, is anything the matter?", I said, "No, there's nothing that we need worry about, it is just that I've got enough money saved up to buy what we need, and we want to get married." He replied, "If I was in your place, I should have waited another year or two, you are doing well at work and at the Mining School, while you are here your hat covers your family, and when you get married, then your troubles begin".

He was right, troubles did begin in the first two or three years, what with short time working, two babies, one or two small strikes, but all the same, we were very happy, it made us both rely on one another, and we pulled through.

Chapter 15

I was very lucky, I obtained the tenancy of a nice house six weeks before our wedding day, and we got it all furnished and fitted up. We were proud of it, it looked so nice and comfortable.[18]

The wedding was a quiet one, but everyone had a good time, plenty to eat and drink, all sorts. We had a carriage and pair of greys to take us and the guests to Church, and the cabby came for me and my brother Albert just after 2 p.m. on Boxing Day,[19] and then went for some of the party from Gertie's home. We were all waiting in the Church for Gertie and her father to come, and the time kept going on and on until it was about ten minutes to three, and the Vicar was getting anxious, as three o'clock was the limit at that time.

**Compliments Slip accompanying
a piece of George and Gertie's Wedding Cake**

Then they came, and we were married before three o'clock. Being Boxing Day, the cabby had been to several other weddings, he was nearly drunk, and had taken them the wrong way round, if they had let him go on without pulling him up, they would have been too late. At about 11 p.m. that night, I said to my wife, we had better slip out of the way quietly, and walk up home, so we went and said 'Good Night' to her mother, and of

---

[18] *On his wedding certificate his address is 230 Arbury Road.*
[19] *Although the wedding certificate is dated 27th December.*

course there was the usual flow of tears from both of them, then we went to our 'love nest'. We didn't go away for a honeymoon, in fact, I had spent about all I possessed, except about enough to meet our household expenses for the first fortnight. After another day's holiday at home, I started back to work again, where I got my leg pulled, but my workmates all wished me the best of luck, and they had bought us a good case of cutlery.

Arbury Road, 1900s

Life went along very smoothly, but we were very happy, although we had to be very careful. Money was none too plentiful, as the pits were on short time, but we agreed a fixed household allowance, and I saved what I could out of the rest. It didn't amount to much, but we had always a few pounds to fall back on, when times were very bad, or illness came along. There wasn't any out of work pay, nor sick-pay either, and the Doctors if you need them wanted their fees when they called or when you attended the Surgery, so it was a case of, <u>no money</u>, <u>no Doctor</u>, unless he knew you were straight and would pay later.

In the autumn of 1910, Gertie was expecting her first baby, so I arranged with my fellow stallmen to let me work on days regular, instead of working nights every other week. This made it better for my Little Lady, as she didn't like being on her own at night time.

We had made all the arrangements with the Doctor and the mid-wife, and about six o'clock on Sunday afternoon, November 13, 1910, I had to fetch Mrs. Sherwood, the old midwife, and the struggle began. The old lady was not very strong and could not help Gertie much, and as it often happens with the first child, the pain was terrible. As I stood at the bottom of the stairs[20] listening to my wife moaning and groaning, occasionally crying out with pain, I vowed to myself, never again, if I can help it, (but how soon we forget).

After about three hours, I went up to the bedroom door, and asked the old lady how things were, and was everything all right? She said yes, wait a bit longer. But I didn't wait, I went to the Doctor, and he came straight away, he wasn't in the bedroom more than five minutes, and the baby was born. I wish that I had fetched him at seven o'clock instead of being ruled by the old lady, but you are not supposed to do so until she told you. Dr W. Mason came downstairs, and said "Well, Mr Clarke, you're better off than I am, you've got a fine bonny son". I thanked him, and we had a drop of brandy each.

When I was allowed, I went in to see them, but the baby didn't interest me a lot, I only wanted to see if my Little Lady was all right. When she looked at me and smiled, I knew she was all right, and I felt on top of the world. The baby looked bonny and strong, and my wife was my chief

---

[20] *In the 1911 census, this was 144, Arbury Road, a '5 roomed house'.*

concern, and all was done to make her happy and comfortable. She was the one thing that I thought about from the time I left to go to work until I got home again.

My brother-in-law's girlfriend Elsie looked after her in the house, while I was at work. The baby did not thrive very well the first two or three months, my wife tried to breast-feed him, but it didn't suit him, so a friend of ours advised us to try Robinson's Patent Barley, with the milk from one cow only, and this was a success. From a crying, puny infant, he changed into a bonny, contented little chap, full of life and smiles, and slept sound as a rock. After being disturbed every night for eight or nine weeks, it was grand to get a good night's rest.

We named him Sidney Thomas, and called him Tommy, and everything went smoothly for several months, then Tommy had a severe attack of sickness and diarrhoea. We called our own Doctor in, his name was S., he was known as the cold water doctor, and when he had examined Tommy, he said, "Keep him warm, and give him little sips of cold water, everything will soon be alright then".

When I got home from work, my wife told me what the doctor had said, but Tommy was worse, and when I looked at him, it put the 'wind' up me. Just about this time, a new doctor had opened the Surgery close to our own house, so I went at once and fetched him. He was an ex-army doctor, Scotch, and very fiery tempered, short and abrupt. When he saw the child, he asked us why we hadn't called him in sooner, and I told him that Dr. S. was our own regular doctor, but we were not satisfied with his treatment. He said, "It against our code to visit another doctor's case without his permission, but to hell with the code, it's a good job you called me in or you would have lost your baby".

I went across to his surgery, and he gave me some tablets which were to be crushed up, and given in a small quantity of water. I asked him about the fee, and he said, "Never mind the fee now, man, get over to your bairn, and if you want me again, fetch me."

The medicine acted like a charm, sickness and diarrhoea stopped, and Tommy was all right again in a couple of days. We both blessed that doctor. I have never bowed my head, nor bent my knee, to any man, but I could have gone down on my knees for that fiery Scotchman, and blessed him. He did not stay long in our neighbourhood, or he would have been our family doctor, so we had to fall back on the cold water doctor, again.

When Tommy was about 12 months old, we had another slight shock, my wife said that we were going to have another baby, so we had to save all the coppers we could, and make preparations again, but we pulled through all right. This time was much easier for my Little Lady, everything went well, and we became the proud parents of a lovely little girl, with auburn hair, pink cheeks, and blue eyes. She was a beautiful baby, and Tommy was a good-looking, bonny lad, we are proud of them, all my wife's girlfriends envied her, and told her how lucky she was, to have such a nice pigeon pair. We named her Hilda May, and as the months went by she became lovelier, and never ailed a day until the winter of 1912, when she had an attack of Bronchitis, which passed off until the Spring of 1913, and again she had Bronchial trouble. Dr. S. attended her, and gave his usual prescription, cold water, but pneumonia set in, and we lost our lovely little girl.

I always blamed the doctor for this, and as we grew older, we both knew that it was our inexperience, and the doctor's attitude to the case, which caused her to fade away. Poultices ought to have been applied, and the congestion of the lungs eased. I am a strong believer in

Fate, but this wasn't Fate, it was a lack of knowledge on our part, and not enough serious thought and application by the doctor.

My wife never liked the house after this, and although we had got it nicely fitted, and I had made the back, and the garden very pretty, full of rose bushes and other plants, I thought it would be best to make a move.

Chapter 16

We went to a house nearer to Nuneaton, a well built house, but rather dark and gloomy, this is where we made a mistake, we never felt settled and comfortable. We had another short strike at the colliery, and I thought it's time I made a move for a better job, and got out of the rut.

I read in our local paper that Mr H. Watson Smith had gone to Denaby Main Colliery as Manager. He had been my teacher at the Mining School, so I wrote to him asking for a position as Deputy. He replied and offered me a job as Overman Deputy, on the day shift. I accepted his offer, and off I went to Yorkshire on my own, to find a house in Denaby, so that Gertie and Tommy could come and join me.

I got lodgings with a very nice Yorkshire man and wife, Mr. and Mrs. Haigh, where I was very comfortable, Mrs. Haigh treated me like a son. After about three weeks, a good house became vacant, and I obtained the tenancy, sent for my wife and the furniture, and we were together again.

Denaby was only a small mining village, and consisted of a number of large blocks of squalid, dirty looking houses, back to back, no gardens, and nearly all owned by the local Colliery Company. The street where our house was situated was in the best part of the village, the houses were well built, and most of them privately owned. It was several weeks before we got on a level footing, expenses had been very heavy, rail fares, furniture removal expenses, etc., had exhausted all our savings, so we had to start all over again, but I was working seven days a week, and overtime as well, so we soon got on an even keel again.

We were at Denaby about 18 months, and my wife must have felt very lonely at times. I worked seven days a week most of the time, up at 4 a.m., back home at 4 p.m., or a lot later sometimes, I was expected to attend for instruction and practice, at the Ambulance Classes and drill parades, two nights a week. We had to make the most of Saturday and Sunday night, and usually went into Mexborough on the Saturday night to the Music Hall. The only redeeming feature of Denaby was the Co-Operative Society, which paid a dividend of 5/- in the pound, made possible by the profits from an off-licenced store run by the Co-op, which did an enormous amount of business.

Now for a few words about my work at Denaby Main, which at that time, was one of the largest collieries in Yorkshire, along with Cadeby Colliery, owned by the same Company. The manager was Mr H. Watson Smith, a very clever, efficient, methodical man, cold, lacking any consideration, or human feeling for the working man, and he hadn't got a smile, nor any sense of humour, all he wanted was good service, and coal production. Tom Jones, the under-manager, was a big jolly, bluff chap, he never minced his words, (except when he was talking to the manager) and he had a fiery temper when he was roused, or when things went wrong, the air was blue for a time. He was a good, practical, tireless miner, and expected everyone else to be the same. His work was his life, and his hobby as well, so what with him, and the manager, I had my plate full.

The first morning when I landed in the office at the shaft-bottom, Tom was playing 'hell up' with the night deputy, and the old chap took it all, without any back answers. I thought to myself, George, you won't last long here, if he goes on like this, I can see a cussing match developing. He was very patient with me for the first week or two, as it was my first trial as a regular deputy. I thought I was doing all right.

One morning, he came into the office in a raging temper, someone had upset him, and he asked me about the job which he had told me to get done. I said, "I'm sorry, Tom, I forgot all about it." He replied, "Sorry be buggered, you're always bloody well forgetting, why don't you make notes, you won't forget then." My answer, "You're a bloody liar, that's the first time I forgotten anything you've told me". That put the fat on the fire. One word led to another, we had a right good set-to, and he told me, "Look here, you young bugger, you'll soon be finished here if you talk to me like that." I replied, "Don't worry yourself, if you think you are going to boss me around like you do all the rest, you're making a big mistake, I can always earn my living anywhere, work doesn't frighten me, I could go back to where I came from."

After this 'bust up', he took to me, and we became good friends. I made notes, and he had a go at me at times when something had gone wrong, but we used to have a good laugh when it was all over. Good old Tom, he trained me to become a good, efficient deputy, and also, to hold my own with any type of working man.

The last time I saw him was in September 1923. I went to Yorkshire for two or three days for Leger Week, and called to see him. He was under-manager of the new colliery near Doncaster, and doing well. He was still the same, full of his job, all work and worry.

When I had been at Denaby Main about 18 months, the manager, Watson Smith, went round with me on one of his periodical inspections. One or two things didn't suit him, and when we got back to the shaft bottom, he said, "What about the back timber in such and such stall, it ought to have been drawn out." I told him that it wasn't safe to get it out until the packs were on, and this caused a row. He said I thought I knew more than he did, and that rubbed me up the wrong way, so I told him that I knew more about the practical side of mining, even if he was the manager.

This got his hair off, and he told me if I talk to him like that, I would soon be finished. As I was fed up to the teeth, I said, "Don't worry yourself, I'm finished <u>now</u>. For 18 months I've worked more than 70 hours a week, but not a word of praise, or even a thank-you, you can keep your job, I've had enough." Tom, who had stood by me listening to it all, said afterwards, "You silly young bugger, why didn't you bite your tongue, I have to do, many a time, now, what are you going to do?; come and talk it over at my house tonight."

When I got home and told my wife, she said, "Now you've done it, where are we going now?" I told her not to worry, I'll get a job at one of the new collieries round about Doncaster.

Tom gave me a note to give to the under-manager at Bentley Colliery, but when I went there the next day, he was away on his holidays, so I went to Bullcroft Colliery, where they signed me on as 'getter', to work on the nightshift. After obtaining lodgings in Bullcroft Village, I went back home, and fetched my case and pit clothes, left my Little Lady in tears, and went to Doncaster, feeling a bit down in the mouth, and also a bit fed-up. However, things turned out all right, I was moved from one stall to another all the week, 'I was on the market', and the first payday, I had to go to five different contractors for my wages. When I saw the deputy, I told them that I didn't want that sort of a job, so he fixed me up with a decent set of stallmen, and things were better.

Chapter 17

When I had been working at Bullcroft about three weeks, I had a letter from Mr H. S. Witty, the manager of Kilnhurst and Swinton Common Collieries, offering me a position as a deputy. When I went to my interview, he told me that he wanted me to look after a district at the Swinton Common Colliery, which owing to bad management by the under-manager and a deputy, had got into a very poor state, and coal production was getting lower and lower every week. The first World War was on its way, and coal was urgently needed, so he had got to make a change. I accepted the position, on condition that the under-manager was not to interfere with my method of working, and Mr. Witty told me that I would be in full control, wished me the best of luck, shook my hand and said "Good Lad", come and see me again.

For the first two weeks, I went round the district, seeing and hearing all, but not saying much, and the word went around that they had got a 'parson' as boss. Until one day, I was fetched back about half a mile to look at a small fall in one of the stall roads. The stallmen were sitting down looking at it. When I got there, I asked them why they had not shifted it, they said the former deputy would not have paid for the work unless he saw it first, and then he would cut them to the last penny. I played 'hell-up' with them, told them that I had come to get the coal out, and that I was going to have it out. Whatever they did extra, I would see that they were paid for it, but that nothing must hinder the production of more coal.

This spread round the district like lightning, and by talking to the men, getting on the right side of them, paying them well for all the 'odd work', and sticking to my promise to Mr Witty, the output of coal began to increase. I doubled the output in six months. One of my best helpmates was the afternoon deputy, Arthur Winstanley, and the Corporal, Charlie Hutchinson, who did his best for me.

My Little Lady was much happier when I was at home again, and I soon obtained another house at Rosehill, Rawmarsh[21], which is closer to my work, so off we went again, and glad to leave Denaby. We were much happier and a lot more comfortable in our new abode, it was only a small house, but very bright and cheerful, compact and well fitted up, and my wife was more contented than she had been for months.

Gertie with Tommy, 1916

Tommy was growing up and looked well, full of mischief and fun, he kept his mother busy looking after him. We

---

21 *97, Main Street, Rawmarsh*

liked the little Yorkshire village, and the people were very friendly and helpful, so we soon settled down. Rotherham was about 2 miles away, we went there on Saturday nights, shopping, and then to the Music Hall, where we saw most of the top stars of the day.

I wrote to Amos Jones, and told him that I could fix him up in a good job. He replied, and accepted my offer. I went to a house to get him lodgings, and there was a bonny looking young woman living there, the grand-daughter, with a bit of a reputation in the village. After fixing things up with the old lady for Amos to lodge there, the young woman, who had been looking at me all the time, got up and said, "I'll let you out by the front door." It was raining very heavily, so she said, "Take my umbrella, it will keep you from getting wet through, you can bring it back tomorrow night, grandmother will be out then, I want to talk to you, and we can have some fun".

The next night, after I had washed and changed, had my dinner, read the paper, played with Tommy, etc., I said to my wife, "I think I'll take the umbrella back". She replied, "Oh no you won't, I'll take the umbrella back, and you can keep away from that house, two or three of the neighbours have told me to stop you going to that place". Villages are small places, and you never know who is watching you, so I thought it best to pack it up at once.

Old Amos had a good time while he was lodging there. She was a very attractive young woman, and until his wife and family came over, he made the most of his opportunities, and told me all about them.

The first World War was on, and black-outs were enforced, owing to the large steel and wire works at Parkgate and Rotherham, also, the numerous collieries, and armament factories, round about the district. The Zeppelins came over several times, and dropped one or two bombs, but they didn't do much damage, only put the breeze up the people. All the miners had to join up in Lord Derby's Army, in case we were needed, but they never called us up.

After we had been at Rawmarsh a few months, Esther wrote and told us that they were taking over the King William IV Inn, on Coton Road, Nuneaton. This did not interest us much at the time, but it had a big influence on our lives later on, and also that of Gert's parents, upsetting the routine and the peace.

One of my big pals at work was a big chap named Bernard Hartley. He was the deputy on the day shift, we had many a hearty laugh. All the rest of the officials, including the under-manager, were very straitlaced, and couldn't understand what Bernard and I were chuckling about. We sat opposite each other in the under-manager's office for the daily conference, and when something tickled him, or when the under-manager went a bit dreamy, he used to kick my leg, wink, and start me off chuckling or laughing. He was very fond of horse-racing, he liked a pint or two, and enjoyed life to the full. He was also a very good deputy, and knew a lot about practical coal mining, and the methods and customs of the district.

In his younger days he had worked as a pit shaft sinker, and when they were sinking Arley Colliery shafts, he was in charge of the fund which the men paid for a week's supply of meat. One Saturday, when he went to Nuneaton to buy the joint for the Sunday's dinner. he went to some dog racing first. He lost all his money, and the meat money as well, except for three shillings. He bought a cow's head for half a crown, smuggled it into the cook's pantry at night, and went to bed. Next morning when the cook found it, he expected to find a big joint, the H. Bone, so he went to Bernard, and shouted, "I see you brought the meat, but tha's brought the wrong

111

bloody end". They had to have soup for Sunday's dinner, and Bernard went for a walk while they cooled down.

Dad came to see me while I was at Swinton Common. When I met him at Rotherham Station, he had brought his crooked "Harry Lauder" stick[22]. I said, "What the hell have you brought that for, you'll have all the folks in Rotherham staring at you." Dad's answer was, "I know that, I want them to, I haven't been in Yorkshire many minutes, and more people have noticed me in that short time than will notice you if you live here all your life." He enjoyed himself, and sang some of his good old songs when he went for a drink in the pubs.

In 1916, my daughter, Norah, was born.

Norah at 6 months old

---

[22] *Harry Lauder, the popular entertainer, carried a twisted walking stick.*

Norah was a lovely little baby, and my Little Lady was very pleased to have another little girl, she wanted a girl to make up for the loss of Hilda, so she got her wish. My wife's sister, Lizzie, came over to look after her, and stayed with us for three or four weeks. Her husband was in the R.A.M.C.[23], and stationed in Gallipoli at that time, so she was glad to be able to talk to Gertie over old times, they both enjoyed it.

I got on very well with the men under my charge at the Colliery. Yorkshire men are noted for their stubbornness and strength of character, but by using plenty of tact, being pleasant and reasonable, and acting straightforward when it came to the question of paying for work done, I soon gained their respect and goodwill. They would do anything for me within reason, and between us, we kept a regular and consistent output.

We had a rather bad fall which temporarily stopped two of the stalls, and Mr Witty came along to see me. We had quite a long chat, and when I told him what we intended to do to get the stalls going again, he looked at me and said, "How old did you say you were?" I replied, "Twenty eight." He patted me on the shoulder and said, "I thought you were much older than that, anyhow, carry on, you know your job, keep your chin up and that twinkle in your eye, and you'll pull through."

In the spring of 1917, Dad wrote to me and said that he could fix me up in a good stall if I wanted to come back to Nuneaton, and as my wife was getting a bit homesick, she missed her mother and the rest of the family, I accepted the offer, and put my notice in. When I went to see Mr Witty, he asked me why I was leaving, and I told him about my wife's wishes. He said he was very sorry to lose me, that if an increase in wages would make me change my decision he would give me a substantial rise.

---

[23] *Royal Army Medical Corps*

I thanked him for all that he had done for me, but I said I couldn't accept his offer, the happiness of my wife was more important to me than money.

He was a grand old man, and it was a pity that in his later days, I heard that he was forced to accept a position of much lower standing. Still, as we grow older, we have to learn to accept these changes, youth will have its way, and when youth has ability as well, 'old 'uns' have to give way.

**George and Gertie
with Tommy and Norah, 1916**

Chapter 18

I went back to Nuneaton, and stayed with Dad and Mother for a few weeks, and my wife joined me a week or two later, until we found a very nice house[24], and we were happy again in our own abode, and back home again.

Mollie, Tommy, and Norah, 1919

I did very well for several months and life went along very smoothly, though I was working very hard, and continuing with my technical classes. Mother used to call to see us very often, and told us that Dad often complained of feeling tired. Later on he had to have time

---

[24] *26 Arbury Road*

off on several occasions. Mr Stapleton, the under-manager, asked me to take over so that Dad could take things easy for a time, he said it wouldn't affect his wages, so I left the stall and started as a deputy again.

I kept the district in good order and the output up, looked after my Dad, and everything was going well, until Mr Stapleton asked me to take over another district, that was going from bad to worse, but he thought I might improve things, and that I wouldn't lose anything if I accepted his offer. I did so, and in a few months, made the district better, and increased the output.

But the war had made the man-power question very acute, and the coal face men had to be moved where the best seams were being worked, so my district was closed down, and I had to start as a stallman again. This was in the year 1920. After several months hard work, with Amos Jones, and two other good men as fellow stallmen, I had paid the deposit on my house, and still had about £90 in the 'old box' upstairs, and we felt on top of the world. We were now the proud parents of three very nice children, Tommy aged ten, Norah aged four, and Mollie aged two, who was born the same year that the World War ended, 1918. She was a bonny baby, and never gave us any trouble from the time she was born.

When the War ended in 1918, the usual clap-trap was 'dished' out by the politicians, the National newspapers, and the leading Church dignitaries. They all said that this was the War to end all Wars, and nothing was to be gained from War, except misery, poverty, food shortage, destruction of property, to say nothing of the loss of human lives.

For the first few months, nothing happened to upset the working classes, except the cost of living, which rose sharply. Butter was 5/- per pound, eggs 6d. each, bacon and potatoes very scarce, meat was very dear, but bread was still good, and the price was kept at a reasonable level by the aid of subsidies, so bread was the main item in the ordinary man's daily food supply. Even beer was short, most of the pubs only opened about three days a week, and cleared all their stock in that time, some of them only opened at weekends.

Then the Tory Government and Big Business got going. The 'Geddes Axe'[25] began to be used, and the working classes soon realised the value of Tory promises, "a land fit for heroes to live in": men would be demobilized from the Services without any planning or preparation for their re-employment, disabled men were very badly treated, and had to form bands, and groups, to play and sing in the streets for coppers, in order to live. The Civil Services, School Teachers, Municipal Employees, etc., had very big cuts in wages, and thousands were sacked, and thrown on the Labour Market. The subsidy paid to the Coal Owners was withdrawn, and the result was the stoppage of the 1/- per day War Bonus, and notice to the effect that wages would be cut drastically, take it or leave it.

One of the clauses in the Peace Treaty was that Germany was to pay a large part of War Damage Compensation, with coal exports to France, Belgium, and even to Britain, and countries that we had been supplying, this gave the Coal-Owners a good excuse to back up their wage cutting demands.

---

[25] *To pay for the First World War government expenditure and taxation rapidly increased. Taxation per head per annum was £18 in 1919, £22 in 1920, and £24 in 1921. In 1913-14 the Civil Service and Revenue Departments cost £81m, and in 1921-22 they cost £591m. The National Debt and other Consolidated Fund Services increased over the same time from £37m to £360m. The Prime Minister David Lloyd George appointed Lord Geddes as head of a committee in August 1921, with the brief of cutting cost (the Geddes Axe). Geddes implemented £52m of cuts from the budget for 1922-23. One consequence was that an estimated 25% of public sector jobs were lost.*

In the early part of 1921, the Miners came out on strike, the Coal-Owner's demands were getting more drastic every week, and the Government were behind them, which made matters worse.

I was out of work 21 weeks, and our nest egg of £90 just kept us going steadily during that time. You may say to yourself, why not get another job?, but there were no jobs to be obtained, and we were only "those dirty, grabbing miners". The pits were open for work on the Owner's terms, and it was our own fault if we were out of work.

One of the best speakers that I heard during this time was A. J. Cooke. He flayed the Coal-Owners, and the Tory Government, right and left, I often wondered why he was allowed so much freedom of speech, he would have been put in detention now, as a dangerous Communist agitator. The strike fizzled out, we went back to work, on the same terms which we were offered to us when we came out, and the Tories were on top again.

During the time I was at home, I was busy on my garden and allotment, repairing and enlarging my fowl pens, and doing odd jobs about the house, in addition to helping my wife with the general housework, and looking after the children. It was lovely weather all months we were away from work, but after about the twelfth week, all our stock of coal had gone, and we needed fuel for washday and cooking. So I went along with some more miners to where the coal outcrops were, and we got about two barrows full each, but this privilege was denied us owing to it being abused, so we had to look somewhere else.

The woods were not very far away, so I got up very early two mornings a week, Tommy went with me, we gathered some bundles of old wood which kept us going, and the early morning air was glorious.

119

Mollie, Tommy, and Norah, early 1920s

We had some very happy times, although we knew that the nest-egg was getting less and less, and that there was no way to stop this, until the strike finished. When the news came through that we were to report for work again, we were about on the last two or three pounds, and on the last week before I started again, my wife came to me one morning and said, "George, we shall last a bit longer, you have won £5 in a Limerick competition, perhaps our luck has changed".

Chapter 19

She was right, it did change. After about 10 days back at work, I was on the night shift, and there was a very bad fall of roof, which knocked me out, and smashed my right leg very badly.[26] There were no proper ambulance facilities at that time, and I was taken to the hospital in the colliery horse and trap, and for a few days I was so faint from the loss of so much blood I didn't know where I was, there wasn't any blood transfusion service then. I must have been half-way between life and death, but I pulled through, thanks to good nursing by Nurse Belliss and her staff, and Dr. Woods' attention. They were untiring in their efforts, and nothing was too much trouble. I was in hospital 14 weeks, and the weather was glorious all that time, in fact, there was a water shortage, and water had to be brought to the hospital in the municipal water wagons.

During this time, my Little Lady had to manage, and keep her end up on the magnificent sum of 30/- per week, and one load of coal every two months instead of every month, Coal-Owners generosity and consideration for good service?

Eventually I landed home, and used a pair of crutches until my leg got stronger, when I was then able to walk with the aid of a couple of strong walking sticks.

My wife's parents had been the tenants at the King William IV Inn, Coton Road, Nuneaton, for two or three years, having taken over from their daughter, Esther, while her husband was in the Army. Owing to the Coal Strike, unemployment, and other causes, they were in low water, and could not carry on, and asked my wife several times if I would like to take over.

---

[26] *The accident happened early on a Saturday morning, and George was trapped for over 48 hours.*

As my leg got stronger, I was able to get about more easily, but the problem of making a good living wage was always at the back of my mind. I knew that working at the coal-face again was out of the question, as the accident so badly crippled me. Walking and knocking about a large district as deputy was more than I could do.

The wages paid to compensation men, who worked on or about the surface of the mine, were very poor, and the compensation in general was scandalously low, and reduced, or stopped altogether, if there was any loophole that the Coal-Owners could take advantage of. Men, women, or children could starve, there was neither consideration nor sympathy.

After about three months at home, I was in the garden, and my wife came to me and said that her mother had written to say that if I wanted to take over the tenancy of the King William IV it would have to be done at once, as they had given their notice in to the brewery to quit as soon as possible. When my wife had finished telling me the news, I said, "Well, this is our chance, do you want to go there, we might do well, and at least, we ought to make a good living." Her reply was, "I am willing to go, if you want to, but Dad and Mother have been in trouble all the time they have been there, and it has never been a really good place."

I decided to have a go, and talk the matter over with my brother Albert, who promised to lend me the money necessary to cover the valuation, and the initial expenses, etc. I then went to see my father-in-law, and got all the details from him about his financial affairs, and a note from him stating that he was willing for me to take over the Licence and Tenancy.

Next, I went to see the Receiving Manager of the Burton Brewery Company, a big, strong, good-looking man named Rudgard, (the company was actually in liquidation, and he had been promoted from the position of Head-Brewer, to that of Receiving Manager). He was a good, shrewd businessman, and when I went in to see him, he looked me up and down, weighed me up well, and told me to sit down. I gave him my father-in-law's note, and he said "So you want to take over ? Are you financially able to do so, it will mean several hundreds of pounds, there's no stock whatever, and the first consignment of goods will have to be paid for before delivery." "That will be all right", was my reply, "I can stock the place well, and still cover the valuation, etc." Mr Rudgard said "That's good, what has been the trouble with Mr Brooks, I know times have been hard, but they ought to have made a living."

I told him that there were too many pulling at the old folks, in addition to the effects of the Coal Strike, short time, and unemployment, they hadn't had a fair chance, it wanted someone to put the screw on. He said, "Well, Mr. Clarke, I did really intend to take the tenancy of the pub out of the family altogether, the last five or six years has been nothing but trouble through one thing or another, but now I've had a good talk to you, I think you will be the right man for the job. This is conditional, on the understanding that you live there on your own with no hangers on".

I promised to do this, and signed the agreement. He shook hands with me and said "Now, young man, you are going into business for the first time, take things steady, don't indulge in the strong drinks, stick to a drop of good beer, that won't harm you, and a last word of good advice, watch your till, don't let anybody else riddle it". The Burton Brewery's Beer and Ale was grand stuff at that time, and no doubt Mr Rudgard knew his business. I have never tasted or seen beer like it since, perhaps that was why the company went into liquidation, the quality was too good for the money.

Chapter 20

This was one Thursday, March, 1922, and when I got back to Nuneaton, I called in the King William IV and told the old folks what had transpired, and the conditional agreement. This upset them a bit, but I told them it was the only way out. It was arranged between us for them to move into our house, as we had moved our furniture into the King William IV, and I would settle the cost. We moved into the pub on the next Monday, and thus we began another episode, which started well, and we did really good business for the next two or three years. Then the slump came and hundreds, nay thousands, of small businessman lost all they possessed, through no fault of their own.

However, before this happened, we had some very enjoyable and exciting times. The work was long and exacting, dirty and disagreeable at times, but we enjoyed the life, and it is a business that keeps you on your toes, full of ups and downs, fun, misery, and everything that makes what we call life.

The news that I had obtained the tenancy of the pub pleased the members of my family, and also some of my old friends and workmates, who had been wondering what my next job was going to be, and they wished me the best of luck. The transfer of the Licence took place straight away, the valuation completed, and I became landlord of the King William IV in March 1922.

The first thing for a publican to learn is how to look after the cellarwork, so that the beer, ales, wines and spirits are all ready, and in good condition for serving. It was very important in those days, money was short, and the public expected good value for their money. I had gained a lot of experience during the time we were at the Turks Head, Bilston, and this came in very useful after a few hints from my father-in-law, and help from my brothers-in-law. Two of my brothers-in-law were temporarily out of work, so I found them some spare time work, cleaning the place up, whitewashing the cellar, stables, lavatories, storehouses, etc., and clearing all the rubbish, etc., from the back yard.

George's brothers-in-law
From left: Fred, Levi, Sidney and Percy Brooks

My wife, her sister, Mabel (who was staying on with us as barmaid)[27], with the help of a good charwoman, soon got the living quarters and bedrooms straightened up, and the old pub was thoroughly spring cleaned from attic to cellar, and we settled down to a new life.

The next thing to do was to get to know the customers, and encourage them to talk about the good service and first-class quality of the beer, ale, bottled goods, wines and spirits, and the trade began to pick up, increasing gradually each week, as we became more known and people enjoyed calling in to see us. I engaged a pianist to play on Friday, Saturday, and Monday night, and we did

---

[27] *Mabel was paid ten shillings a week, including full board.*

really good business on these nights, although expenses were rather heavy, and the accommodation too small to offset these.

Dick Richardson, pianist at the King William

The first week of my tenancy, I went up to the Colliery office to draw my compensation money. The cashier told me that it was stopped, I asked the reason, and he said that as I have got another job as a publican there was none for me. I said "That's quick work, I only took the place over this week, and the temporary licence was only granted to me on Monday, how do I know whether it is going to pay or not?" He replied, "That's your lookout, not ours, my instructions were to stop payment." I consulted my solicitors, and they advised me to put in a claim for a lump sum to settle the matter up. This dragged on for some months, but I eventually received the princely amount of £100, which included all the back pay due.

There were no free legal advisers to take your case up, and the Unions were not strong enough financially to back compensation cases up, so that I had to make the best of a bad deal, and accept the miserable settlement, to make up for becoming a cripple for the rest of my life. Thank God, owing to the efforts of the Labour Party and the Trade Unions, compensation is now paid on a much better scale, and based on what the worker might have earned in his working life, had he not been injured. These conditions would never have been obtained if the Tory Party and Big Business had kept their power and control, but their claws were cut, and the working classes got better treatment.

George in the garden at the King William

This money came in very useful at that time. My wife and I both had a good supply of new clothes, the children were well fixed up, and the household linen, etc., replenished. Tommy was now going to the Grammar School, and Nora went to Miss Mariott's Private School.[28]

---

[28] *Miss Marriott's was a one room school taking no more than 20 pupils. It stood until the 1980's opposite Nuneaton Town Hall.*

My wife also had a few days holiday at Blackpool, which she needed after all the turmoil and stress that she had undergone during the previous months. It did both her and the children a lot of good.

As I stated before, Mabel, my wife's youngest sister, stayed on as a barmaid. She was a very attractive, lively girl, and besides being very helpful in the business, she was very fond of the children, and a big help to my Little Lady. She was full of fun, and when we were in the bar together, made my wife and me almost choke with laughter at the remarks she made about some of the customers, not very loud, of course.

Mabel Brooks, 1926

One customer who usually came in at week-ends wore an old bowler hat, which he must have bought in the

Victorian Age. It had gone green, Mabel would mutter to me when he came up to the counter, "Look, George, two penn'rth of brim, and a bob's worth of hat, the bugger's gone mouldy."

She was a good help to me during the first few weeks, she knew all the old regular customers, and told me which ones could be trusted to pay up.

**George, Mabel, Norah and Mollie
in the garden at The King William**

I got two or three of the customers, miners who were on short time, to lay a lawn at the rear of the back yard, and enclose it with rustic fencing. Three rustic bowers and shelters were made, and the borders filled with rambler roses and shrubs. Terraced stone steps were laid from the yard to the lawn, and I bought three large garden vases, which later were full of geraniums and other flowers.

During the summer months, quite a lot of new customers came at week-ends, to look at the garden and sit in the rustic shelters while they had a drink or two. The Licensing Magistrates would not allow music, or we could have had dancing on the yard, which was quite a good size.

The prices of the goods at that time were - Strong Old Ale 8d, Best Bitter 7d, and Mild Ale 6d and 5d, all per pint. Spirits and Wines were good and cheap. The most popular drink was 'Mixed', half 'Old' and half 'Mild'. The old hands always watched you, when you were filling their glass, to see that they had their proper share out of the 'Old' tap. We were very busy, I used to look at my wife and Mabel, and mutter to them, "Go easy on the 'Old' pull, the 'Mild' is in good condition". They would reply, "We know, you needn't tell us again."

The outdoor trade was very poor at first. A few hundred yards from our own pub there was another pub which was on the corner of a temporary road which led to a large number of streets, all potential customers, this pub was doing an enormous amount of outdoor trade. I knew this publican was very keen on the measure, more under than over, so when I served outdoor, I always gave a little over, not more than a good spoonful, and told my wife and Mabel to do the same. Our outdoor trade soon began to increase, and the other publican's sales were reduced by two barrels per week, but it also made a difference to the sale of his cigarettes. The public are fickle and easily tempted.Most of my regular bar customers in the week-time were miners, some of them ex-army men who served in the first World War, and one or two of the older ones had served in the South African War. Some of them were real 'Old Bill' types, and the yarns they used to spin were funny, queer, interesting, and sometimes crude and obscene.

Four of the young ones came in during the second week I was there, and ordered four pints of 'Mixed', when I had filled them and put them on the counter, they looked at one another, and said "It's Jack's turn to pay this time", Jack said, "I know it ain't, it's his turn." They passed it on from one to the other for a minute or two, and I twigged they were trying me out. They started to pick the glasses up, but I put them under the counter first, and said, "Make your bloody minds up, which one is going to pay, and then you can have the beer." They all laughed, paid up, and from then on they were regulars.

A favourite tryout of some of the ex-army men was the 10/- note trick, and the 2/- piece trick. If they thought the person behind the bar was nervous, or a bit green, they would come up for a drink when it was a busy time, put a 10/- note down, and when given the correct change, dispute it and say it was a one pound note they'd handed over. It only worked when the person in charge was green, bewildered, or frightened to speak up. The 2/- piece trick was to pay with a 2/- piece, and then claim the change for a 2/6 piece. I stopped this sort of trouble at once. All of us when we were serving, placed the 10/- notes and 2/- pieces on the top of the till until the customers had gone away from the counter. If there was any dispute, we merely pointed to the note or coin, and said, "That's what you gave me."

At that time, competition was keen, and the publican had to keep the beer and ale in good and sparkling condition if he wanted to keep his customers. I have known some of the scrounging type, who have perhaps filled their 'slate' full at a pub, go in and order a pint, and then hold it up to the light, and say "This is a bit cloudy, it's clearly gone off." All the other customers would do the same, and think the beer was not up to proper standard, drink up, and move on to the next pub. These scroungers would also say to their pals and to everybody else who was in ear-shot, "I don't go in So-and-So's the stuff's not worth drinking." So publicans had to be on their mettle, to counteract these statements by these mischief makers.

Chapter 21

However, we overcame all these little trials and troubles, it was a pleasure to open up, and see the customers come bustling in, and give them satisfaction.

Gertie with Mabel outside The King William

One of my regulars was an ex-soldier in the first War, Alec Ensor. He was a natural born comedian, and I am sure if someone in the Music Hall world had taken him up, given him some training, and polished him up a bit, he would have made the 'top of the bill' grade as a comedian. He was a proper 'Bairnsfeather' 'Old Bill'[29] type, and could mimic, imitate dozens of characters, especially Army Officers, and Non Commissioned men, both in his methods of speech and actions. Whenever he was in the bar, he kept the company in roars of laughter and good spirits. I treated him to many a drink, it kept the company together. Several of the other customers could tell some good yarns, but they were not in the same street as Alec.

One young ex-Army man was G.P., a very nice chap when he was sober, but when he had been on the booze over the week-end, he became very nasty tempered and would fall out with anybody. When he was in France in the first World War, he was put in charge of a number of Chinese Coolies, who were helping with the work in the trenches. George got drunk one day, and when he was making his way back to his tent saw three of these coolies asleep in the sun. Creeping quietly up to them he cut all their pigtails off. For days after, when he had sobered up, he went about in fear and dread, as the coolies were threatening to knife whoever had done it. The pig-tails are the coolies' pride and joy, and to lose them was a terrible blow.

One day when George was hungry, he saw the company officer's batman cooking a good meal. When it was ready, George rushed up to the batman, and told him he was wanted very urgently in another section. George pinched the lot, ham, sausages, eggs and tomatoes. He said, "What a meal, well worth being put in clink for." He was one of my best customers, and always brought his friends and relations to see us, I knew how to humour him when he was in one of his bad moods.

---

[29] *A popular English cartoonist of World War I was Captain Bruce Bairnsfeather, and one of his cartoons depicts two British soldiers under shell fire in a shell hole on the Western Front. One says to the other: "Well, if you knows a better 'ole, go to it!"*

Another customer was a little hump-backed man named Gunn, a bookie's runner, who usually shifted all round the bar, from seat to seat. Sometimes I said to Mabel, "Have you dusted the seats in the bar ?" and she usually replied ", No it won't matter, Gunny will polish them all with the arse of his corduroy trousers."

**Norah and Mollie on a hayrick
at Stretton Fields Farm**

My brother-in-law, Levi, was a sergeant in the Royal Warwick's, and when he was in France, the sub lieutenant in charge of his company was a young, nervous chap who was fresh to the job, and relied on Levi to pull him through. They were detailed one day to march some miles to the front-line trenches to relieve another section, it was getting dusk, and after a bit of

134

rest and a meal, the officer lined the men up, gave the order, and the men started on the march. Levi said very quietly to the young sub, "Sir, we are going in the wrong direction we shall soon be back at the base, instead of at the front-line." The sub's reply was, "Shut up, Sergeant, I know what I'm doing, and another day or two away from that 'hell-hole' will do us both good."

Norah and Mollie outside the King William, with Gertie and Mabel inside

One dark night some weeks later, the same young officer and Levi were in the front line of trenches, and were detailed to take out a raiding party. When they were all ready to go, the officer unscrewed his flask, told Levi to have a good swig, emptied the flask himself, and said, "Go on, Levi, take the lead and I'll follow you." Levi replied, "But, Sir you are supposed to lead, in a raid like this." The young lad looked at Levi, gulped, and said "Go on, Sergeant, you're a good chap, and take the lead, but I will be close behind you." Levi told me that after that night the sub was his best friend, and made a really brave officer. He also told me that some of the old timers said to the men, when they were going on these raids, "Get back as soon as you can, we've got some fresh trousers ready for you, you'll need 'em." When he joined up, he was a raw young lad, but when he came out of the Army after the war was over, he was a full grown man, strong and reliable, but it made him too fond of the booze.

Our 'old ale' was very potent, and one of my middle-aged women customers was very fond of it, and sometimes had a drop too much. She came in one Monday morning, laughing and giggling, and said, "George fill me a half of 'Old', I hope it won't serve me like it did yesterday, I had a drop too much then. When I got home, me and the old man had our dinner, and then I went to bed. It was dark when I woke up, I got up and when I got downstairs, the old man was sitting by the fire reading the paper. I went into the scullery, washed my face, waddled back into the kitchen with the frying pan and the bacon. The old man looked at me, and said, 'What the hell are you going to do now?' I told him I was going to cook his breakfast, and he said 'You silly old bugger, it's still Sunday night, not Monday morning.' " There was no doubt about it, our 'old' was very strong.

Tom McDonagh was one of my regulars. When he came out of the Army, he was a good boxer and had won several heavyweight contests in India. Six feet tall, well made, he ought to have got amongst the 'top notchers', but the booze, and loose living took it out of him, and he never got anywhere. Some of the local sportsmen fixed up a contest with a Bedworth bruiser named Jack Henton and Tom reckoned it would be a walk-over. The contest took place one Saturday afternoon at Bedworth, on a boxing platform in a field, and several hundreds of people were there. When they got into the ring, Tom was in his corner, very quiet, looking rather worried. Henton, on the other hand, was prancing about on his toes in the other corner, flexing his muscles, pulling himself up and down the ring-side ropes, and shouting to his pals, "I'll kill the bugger, I'll murder him, I'll knock him out of the ring." This put the breeze up Tom, and he was beaten before they started.

It was a marathon race for two or three rounds, Henton chasing Tom all round the ring, landing heavy blows whenever he got near enough, eventually landing one that nearly knocked Tom out of the ring, and then Tom lay down, and the great fight was over. This lowered Tom's morale so much that he never went in for another contest, although he was a really good boxer.

Another of my customers was "Bluey", a bookie's runner, and he was always up to some game or another. He usually had his bodyguards with him, "Pooley" and Jack, to help him if he got in any trouble.

Bluey told me lots of yarns, and one of them is well worth room here. Bluey, Pooley, and a stable hand, who was very small, and wore riding breeches and leggings, went to a race meeting, and lost all their money except a few shillings. Bluey instructed the other two what they were to do, and then they went into a pub where they could talk, so that the landlord would overhear them. Bluey said to the stable hand, "Well, Mr Griggs, the information you have given us lately has been wonderful, we have made a bundle, I hope you can keep it up." (Mr W. Griggs at that time was a successful Newmarket trainer). He replied, "Of course I can, when my horses are not out to win, I know the others will do so. Mr Poole knows that, don't you, old boy." Pooley said, "Of course I do, Mr Griggs, you are always in the money."

Bluey said by this time the landlord was cocking his ears, and getting interested, and said to them, "Come

The King William IV
From left: Mabel, Mollie, Norah and George

into my private room, I want to talk to you." He took them into the room, bought them a drink, and said "Can I come in on this ?" Bluey said, "If Mr Griggs is willing, we can let you know the 'goods', but it will cost you a fiver for four good things." The landlord bit, and they were in the money again.

Jack "Feet" Moreton was another character, he derived his nickname from being the possessor of a pair of very large feet, and also being very splay-footed. When he was in the presence of some strangers, he would always pull a large cigarette tin out and say, "Would anybody like a cigarette or cigar?" The tin was full of cigarette ends, all sorts, also cigar ends and a half smoked whiffs. His face was one big grin when he opened it and offered them.

One night Bluey, Pooley and Feet came into the Smoke-Room, and after having a couple of drinks each, Bluey and Pooley went out. I went into the room a bit later and saw Feet sitting there, with his hands hand-cuffed behind his back. I asked what was the matter, and he said Bluey had bet him a packet of cigarettes that he couldn't drink a pint of ale with his hands cuffed behind him. I said, "Who's going to unfasten the handcuffs?" He said "Bluey or Pooley, they've only gone up the back, they'll be back in a minute or two." I told Feet that he would have to go home with his hands behind him, as the other two had said "Goodnight" to me, and gone. Poor old Feet had to waddle off with his hands behind him, what a laugh we all had next day.

One Saturday dinner time, round about 1:40 p.m., one of Bluey's henchmen came in very quickly and whispered to me, "Bluey says that you want to have a real good bet on White Flag." Betting was not in my line at that time, and at closing time, the runner came to me and said, "Did you get a good bet on it?" I told him I hadn't touched it. And he said, "You're a bloody fool, it had won the 1.30." It had, at 8 to 1.

We had a very busy time all the summer months, but we were very happy, and my Little Lady looked very much better. Freedom from financial worries and enjoyable company makes a big difference to the outlook on life, and is a good tonic.

Norah and Mollie

My Dad was wearing well, but Mother had a bad attack of Influenza, and later developed Neuritis in her neck and head. Poor old Mother suffered agonies for several months and then 'passed on'. It makes one wonder why anyone like her, who had always been helpful and willing to do everything in her power to relieve the sufferings of others, should end life in such terrible pain. We all did what we could for her, but it was of no avail and Medical Science was still backward.

Dad went to live with my brother Albert, and later came to stay with us, for several weeks, and we did what we could to help him bear his great loss. He only realised Mother's worth when he had lost her. Something we are all apt to do.

**Gertie's father Levi Brooks
outside the King William**

Chapter 22

We did a very good business all the year, and at Christmas time we were very hard worked, but the turnover justified it, and I felt on top of the world. During 1923, four old cottages came up for sale. They were joined to the back of the pub and I thought that sometime they would be needed to extend the premises, so I arranged an overdraft at my bank and bought them, and later another cottage on the front, which I converted into a shop, as the tenant wished to start up in business.

The purchase of these old cottages was alright at the time, and I had hoped, with the aid of the brewery to make a foot road from the rear of the pub into another block of streets, which would have doubled or trebled our trade.

But it didn't materialise, lack of help and funds stopped it, or we might have been in clover. Such is life, some can scheme and plan, and get 'nowt', while others act like bloody fools, and everything goes right for them and the money just falls into their laps.

Just about this time the Geddes Axe was coming into operation. The Tories were backing up Big Business in their efforts to break the Trade Union movement by means of shortage of employment, men being thrown out of work, on the dole, with the means test being applied, and the dole stopped on the moment, if the person gave the slightest indication that he or she was not genuinely seeking work.

The markets and shops were beginning to be flooded with German and Japanese goods. Also the Czech boot and shoe factories (financed by British and American capital) were flooding the country with their goods, and our factories, producing better class goods, were on short time.

The Socialist policy was only just beginning to grow, and get favourably noticed by the rank and file, but only a very small number had to pluck up the courage to speak up and expound the benefits which the ordinary working class men and women would enjoy under a strong Labour government. In fact, it took several years of mass unemployment and misery before the people realised it was all due to the don't care attitude and bad planning of the Tories, which kept them in a state of bare existence.

I didn't try to ram my ideas down my customers' throats, but sometimes when there is a debate going on about the country's affairs, they would asked my opinion, or I might butt in, and tell them what I thought a good Labour Government would do under the circumstances.

One of my customers told me that I was doing myself no good by expressing my Socialistic ideas; he said the publican in the next pub was a Councillor and he never expressed any of his political opinions. So I told him that the man who had any guts, courage, and intelligence, was never afraid to express his opinion, and give his views on any subject that came along, providing he did it in a reasonable manner.

Later on in the year, some of the members of the local Labour Party wanted me to stand as a Labour candidate for the ward, but I could not spare the time, so I had to turn it down.

We had some really good discussions in the bar at times. Three or four intelligent men who worked in the works department of the local evening paper made a point of coming in two or three nights a week, and we had talks on politics, world affairs, many other subjects, which of course including racing.

My wife was looking very attractive at this time, and as is usual, received many an admiring glance and the glad eye, from some of the young bloods, and also the older

143

"Don Juans". One in particular, a bachelor, used to come in most nights, and if she was in the bar he would stand up against the counter watching her all the time, and I knew what he was thinking.

From left: Charlotte (Gertie's sister), Tommy, Charlotte's husband Arthur, and Gertie

He came in one night, and the bar happened to be empty for a time. He talked to me and my Little Lady for a few minutes, and then he said, "George, what would you say if I asked your wife to go to the pictures with me some night?" My wife looked at me and winked, so I told him, "In the first place, I don't think that she would go with a bugger like you, and if you did, when you came back, either you or I would get a bloody good hiding." He gave a sheepish smile, emptied his glass and went out. He didn't come in again.

Another middle-aged widower used to sit with his pint, and his eyes were on her most of the time when she was in the bar. I guessed what he was thinking, but he never said anything so it didn't matter.

**George's family in the early 1920s
From left: Tom, George, a headless Norah,
Mollie, Gertie, and Mabel**

My wife took the wind out of my sails one day, it was when the Royal Agricultural Show was held at Nuneaton. I went to see the Show, and in one of the tents there was a voluptuous, good-looking blonde, who was giving a demonstration with a new kind of vegetable peeling knife. I bought one and took it home. The same night, I went to serve a customer who had come into the smoke room, and to my surprise, it was the blonde. She ordered a Worthington, and as trade was rather slack at the time, we had a few minutes of very enjoyable conversation.

She had been all over the country demonstrating and selling different kinds of kitchen devices.

When my wife came in, she took over the conversation, and the blonde asked her if she could stay to supper and pay for it, of course, when we closed, as she did not fancy having any at the place where she was staying, and my wife agreed. We had a very good supper, a drink or two after, and then the blonde went to her lodgings. She came in again the next night and when my Little Lady saw her, she looked at me and said, "George, my lad, there isn't going to be any supper, nor stopping after time tonight." I said, "Why, my dear, there's nothing wrong and it's the last day of the show, and she is on her travels again tomorrow." Her reply was, "A good job too, I saw the gleam and the sparkle in your eyes, and I am not going to let you make a fool of yourself. I know what she's after, she will be borrowing a few quid, and you would be silly enough to fall for it"

One morning, there were no customers in, a rather young, good-looking gypsy woman came in and tried to sell me some clothes pegs. I didn't buy any, so she said, "Let me tell your fortune, it will only cost you a silver shilling." After some persuasion I consented and we went into the smoke room, and she crossed my hand and her own with the shilling I gave her. She told me all the usual rigmarole, and then finished up with an unusual saying looking me straight in the eyes and smiling; she said, "Keep your pony in your own stable, you will never have any trouble then, and you won't go wrong." I heard a burst of laughter, my wife and Mabel had been in the bar, listening at the service hatch. The gypsy went, and they pulled my leg for several weeks over the "The Gypsy's Warning", and played it on the piano, time and time again.

146

Norah, Mabel, and Mollie

Opposite our pub there was a well built stone fronted house which became vacant, and was taken over by a rather brisk middle-aged man and his wife, who had two sons. He was employed by a firm which had the advertising rights for the drop curtains in music halls and cinemas in towns all over the country. His job was to canvass the tradesmen, in order to put an advertisement on the drop curtains. The main central positions were easily filled, but the smaller ones on the outer margins took more time to obtain, and it usually took Harry a fortnight to complete filling all the spaces.

He was a good customer, very fond of whisky and bottled ale, and his wife could knock one or two back as well, he was very lively and good company. She was very attractive, smartly dressed, and very interesting to talk to, and her sex appeal made men notice her as soon as she entered the room. Poor old Harry, he was as jealous as the Devil, and could not bear to be away from her, but the nature of his job caused him to be away from home three or four days and nights a week, and during this time his wife would "fly a kite" with anyone she fancied at the time. She didn't overdo things, but liked the company of the opposite sex, especially those who looked well and had plenty of money to throw about.

Harry was always broke after the weekend, and he would come into the pub on Mondays before I opened, borrow a couple of pounds, have a double Scotch or a bottle of ale, treat me to a drink, say where he was going to work, and that he would see me at the weekend. Usually, if it was a new job, he would fill the main positions on the curtain in and day or two, and be back home by Tuesday night, sub half his commission from the firm and then it would take him the all next week to finish the job. He could have completed many of the curtains in a week, but his jealousy was so fierce that he could not keep away from her too long at a time. He asked me many a time if I had seen anybody with her, of course, I told him, "No." The commission for a full curtain made him £20 or more, which was very good money at that time, but having such a wilful, sexy partner prevented poor old Harry from putting all in.

This went on for several months, until one week Harry went one Monday to a seaside town, and his wife must have thought she was safe until the weekend, but Harry came back too soon. He came into the bar when I was getting ready for opening time looking very worried and wild, and said, "George, was my wife in here last night, and was anyone with her?" I told him that she had been in during the early evening, but no one was with her. He said, "I got home about 11 o'clock last night, and the yard door was bolted, I rattled the front door, and eventually my wife came and let me in. I rushed through into the garden and just caught a glimpse of a man getting over the wall at the bottom of the garden. We've had a terrible row, she's taken the boys to her mother's home. I shall put the furniture into storage and pack up with the house, but I am going to try and find that bugger, and if I do, I shall ram this in his heart" and he pulled a carving

148

knife out of his jacket. I thought, I hope he doesn't suspect _me_. He had a good stiff drink, and later on in the day called in and paid me all that he owed, and said goodbye; I never saw them again. Poor old Harry, he would never be able to control her, she was as cunning as a fox, as tempting as Eve, and knew every move in the "come and get me" game.

There was another little woman customer who had a "crush" on a violin player, and asked my wife's sister if she would allow him to give her some lessons on the violin in her front room, one night each week, as her parents had not got enough room. The arrangements were made, and the second week, my wife's sister told us what had occurred. She said, "I listened to the screeching of the violin for a time and then it stopped, I waited several minutes, then went into the room, and they were both on the couch, so I told them to bugger off and do their 'fiddling' somewhere else".

There were one or two women of easy virtue used to come into the pub, but as they did not cause any trouble, nor do anything to annoy anybody on the premises, I always served them with civility. After all, you get some of them in every pub, and very often it is a good policy to be like Nelson, and turn a blind eye in their direction, it's good for trade. One in particular had made an appointment to meet a stranger in the Park one night. It was very dark, and after the business was completed, the stranger said he would have to hurry off in order to catch his train, pushed a folded piece of crinkly paper in her hand, and rushed off. When she got to the first lamp-post, she looked at the expected ten shilling note, but nearly choked when she found she had a neatly folded piece of a potato crisp packet, I'll bet the air was blue for a time. One of her pals told this tale, and she nearly rolled on the floor with laughter, she said that the terms in future would be cash in advance from strangers.

Chapter 23

My son, Tommy, was growing and looking very well and Nora and Mollie, my two daughters, were both going to school, always nicely dressed, looking very clean and pretty, a credit to my "Little Lady."

Mollie, Gertie and Norah, mid 1920s

Trade was still good, especially at the weekends, though the money paid out to pull them in took a lot of the cream off the milk. One day, when I was walking in the park, I thought it would be a good idea to open a refreshment hut and supply tea, mineral waters, ices, sweets, etc., so I wrote to the Parks Committee for permission, and offered to pay a fixed rental for the sole rights for the period from June until the end of September. The agreement was made, and I bought a hut which was placed in a good position in the park, and we fitted it up with all the necessary utensils and stock. We opened up, and Mabel was in charge, business was good for part of the time, but the usual English summer spoilt it, and the results were not very encouraging.

Mabel, mid 1920s

The next year, I wrote to the Committee, and asked for permission to open on Sundays, the park was usually pretty full on this day, and it would have made the venture a good paying proposition, but they would not consent to this, so I let the agreement alone, and someone else took it over.

After two or three years, the Parks Committee had a very nice refreshment pavilion erected, and allowed the person who rented it to trade on Sundays, with the result that he made a good paying concern. Thus my idea was again right, but lack of help and imagination from the people in control spoilt all my plans and ended a good business venture. I let two different people rent the hut, for two different seasons, but they could not obtain permission to open on Sundays so they didn't carry on the next season. From such small beginnings some people with the "Midas" touch, and the luck of the devil, seem to forge ahead, and roll the money in, but some of my ancestors must have been 'Jonahs', not 'Jews'.

There are numerous temptations in the everyday life of a publican and his wife. One of the greatest, especially with young beginners, is the danger of living beyond your income, which is only cured when you are pulled up with a jolt, and brought back to normal. Another one is gambling. The old saying, "slow horses and fast women" are responsible for the failure of many licensees and other business people is quite true. I have known dozens of such cases where the man or the woman, and sometimes both of them, through lack of self-control, have had their heads 'turned' when handling large amounts of money which really does not belong to them, and fallen easy victims to flattery, and an insane desire to cut a big dash, which usually ends in disaster.

I knew one young man and his wife, who were very fortunate to obtain the tenancy of a really good hotel, which in the hands of a careful, level-headed man, would have been a very good investment. But the young man, trying to make himself popular, started taking his

152

customers out on bus outings two or three times a week, spending money paying for drinks, and left his wife to look after an almost empty pub until they landed back when it was nearly closing time. He had always told me that he would have liked my pub, but when he got the chance of one, he was in and out in little over a year.

One Saturday night, we were very busy, and it was about half an hour to closing time. The bar door opened, and a stranger stumbled in. A man made room for him on the seat which ran all round the bar, came up to me with his glass, and asked for two pints. I asked him who was having the other pint, and he said, "My pal, he's just come in." I told him, "That man's having nothing to drink in here, he's nearly drunk, and you ought to have more sense than come for a drink for him."

I had hardly spoken, when in walked a policeman, looked round, especially to see if I had served the man with a drink, so I called him up to the bar, and said, "Next time you see a drunken man about to go into a pub, do your duty in a proper manner, and send him home. Don't wait until you think you'll get a case against the publican for serving a man under the influence of strong drink, you were following the man up the road." One of my outdoor customers had been just behind the policeman, noticed him watching the drunk, then stop outside while the man came in. She came in and told me, but I'd refused to serve the man before I knew what the policeman was doing.

The police, at that time, were very strict about gambling and betting on licensed premises, and the licensee was expected to stop anyone making betting slips out, or the bookie or his runner take any bets. Also customers were not supposed to play a game of dominoes, or darts, and the loser have to pay for a drink or other goods. This was all against the law, and on Saturday midday sessions, a licensee and his assistants had got to be on the alert all the time, as copper's 'narks' and plain clothes men were always mixing with the customers in the crowded bars in one or other of the pubs in order to make a 'case' of it.

Mabel (right) with family friend (and cleaner) Mrs. Ensor

Bluey told me that one Saturday he had taken quite a lot of betting slips in one pub, when he noticed a stranger amongst the customers who looked like a plainclothes man, so he sent one of his henchmen off with the slips. A bit later, when he had only taken about two or three slips, a policeman walked in, and he and the plainclothes man arrested Bluey and marched him off to the police station, where they searched him, but couldn't find any betting slips. Bluey had slipped the two or three slips into his mouth, and swallowed them. So there was no case.

One day a well-dressed man came into the smoke room, had a couple of drinks, borrowed my newspaper, fiddled about with some papers in his briefcase, said "Good Day" and went out. He came in the next day, ordered his drink, borrowed my newspaper again, and opened it straight away at the racing page, and said "Landlord, are you interested in horse-racing?" I replied, "Yes, I like a small bet now and then." He told me he had been doing well for several weeks, he said that he had a brother who was in touch with several of the Lambourn stables, who sent him some very sound information and that if I care to do so, I could share in his bet. I said, "Well, what's the name of the horse, and which race is it in?" He replied," I shall not get the name of the horse until about two o'clock, when I have got to be on the phone to receive it, and then get my bet on." I asked him how much he usually had 'on', he said a fiver, but I could have a couple of pounds on with him if I liked, and he would let me know the result, and the name of the horse, when I opened at six o'clock. I looked at him and said, "Can you see any green in my eye?" He replied, "No, why do you ask me that?" I told him, "I thought you could, but I know a bit more than you thought, when I have a bet on a horse, I like to know it's name before the time of the race, not when the evening paper comes out and it's amongst the also-rans." He picked up his briefcase and off he went, he didn't even say "Good Day", nor come in again.

One cold day, a traveller came into the smoke room at lunchtime. There was a nice fire and he made himself comfortable in a seat close to the fire, ordered half a pint of bitter and asked if he could have threepenny-worth of bread and cheese. I got it for him, and brought a few pickles as well, then he borrowed my newspaper. He sat there for about an hour with the one half pint then said

"Good Day," smiled, and went on his way. This was repeated for the two days that followed. About two weeks later, he came in again about the same time, all teeth and smiles, ordered his half pint of bitter, and could he have some bread and cheese and pickles, and the loan of my newspaper. I said, "And certainly, but it will cost you ninepence instead of threepence." He asked why? And I told him that the last three times he'd been in, he had enjoyed a good lunch, a good fire and a good rest for sevenpence, that the profit on his glass of bitter was one halfpenny, the bread and cheese was a dead loss, plus free pickles. He looked at me a little crestfallen, said "Good Morning", and that was another that I didn't see again.

We had a rather large number at a meeting in the Clubroom one night, and the organiser asked my wife if she would make some cheese sandwiches, and would they fetch them from the living room as they required them, and pay at the same time. A large dish of sandwiches were got ready, placed on the table, and a basin for the money. Sometime later in the evening, my wife came into the bar and said, "George, the sandwiches are all gone." I smiled and said, "That's good, old girl, it'll make you bob or two." She replied, "It won't, some dirty mean blighter has pinched all the money out of the basin while I was out of the room for a couple of minutes."

Every year we had what was known as the 'Wake'. Usually in the late autumn, we put on a very good cold meat spread, with salads and pickles if they were asked for, cakes and biscuits of all kinds, the charge was a bob, and it was for the women customers only.

The tickets sold like hot cakes, and the women had a really good time, especially when the hat went round to collect the coppers for a bottle of whisky so that they could have a tot in their tea. After the tea, most of them made a night of it, and spent the few shillings that they'd saved up for the occasion. It was a Red Letter day for them.

We also put on a good cold spread for the men only, about the same time of year. This was in the early part of the evening, and the charge was two shillings each, as each man was allowed one pint or a bottle of ale free. There was plenty of cold boiled beef, ham and cheese, pickles, celery, and salads. What a 'tuck in' some of the men had: two, and some of them had three, large plates of meat and ham, and then followed this up with large quantities of bread, cheese, and pickles. For some of them, I'll bet, it was their best meal of the year, and then they had a good time for the rest of the night. If any of them were hard up, their pals treated them to a drink or two. I always had a good pianist for both these events, and someone was singing, or they were all chorus singing, until closing time. There was plenty of hard work for all of us, and we made no profit, but it kept the customers together, and made the pub more popular.

Owing to the position of the pub, it was rather out of the way, and the others each side of ours were much nearer to some very thickly populated streets, so that we had to attract our customers by our personal attention, good service, good beer, and popular music. And thus we got a good share.

Chapter 24

The popular daily papers did not give such good racing news like they do at the present time, although some of them did make it one of their items, and this made some punters try the tipsters, who were advertising in a big way in the Sunday papers. Most of them were no good at all, and women, with their intuition, could find more winners sticking a pin in the list of runners.

One of these famous tipsters was M.P., who had offices in Piccadilly, with a great banner across the front, and his name in very large letters. His terms were, the odds to one pound for each winner, I sent to him for a trial wire, and he sent 16 successive losers, although some of them did get placed, but they were all red hot first or second favourite, and you can't make much money out of those. The next wire he sent gave a winner and the day after, he sent a letter asking for the odds due, viz., thirty shillings, which of course, he received ? What do you think?

Another tipster was advertising as F.F., and I think this man did get hold of some good stable information. He usually specialised in handicap races, and the horse that he sent out once a week, very seldom won, and often this horse would be engaged in the same race as his next selection, and more often than not, romp home at very good odds.

Old 'Rog' was one of the biggest bookmakers in the town, and he had worked up quite a large connection, all round the outlying districts. He started as a young man, making a 'book', with a limit of threepence each bet, and by good planning, and a clear calm outlook, he increased his business, so that he could accept very large debts without any fear.

He told me once, that in his early days, he often went to Leicester Races, but only to try and make a fiver. His method was to lay enough on the favourite in the first race to win this amount. If this came up, he packed up and left the course, he said that he didn't stop to let the bookies have it back again.

Leicester Race Meeting at that time was noted for winning favourites, especially in the first or last race. If Roger failed in the first race, he increased the amount of his next bet, so that it would cover the amount he had lost, and also win his fiver. He told me that he never had a losing day. My wife and I went to Leicester Races several times, and had a good days' enjoyment, though I can't say I was as lucky as old Rog. If I won a bit, I always let the bookies have some of it back, and once or twice they had the lot.

One day when I was there, in the Silver Ring, as it was called then, I stood close to two Jews, they had had a 'plunge' on Steve Donohue's mount, and he had got beaten by a short head. I don't know whether Steve's ears were burning or not, but the expression and language that those two Jews turned out were enough to scorch him. I was standing close to the rails down the course, to watch the horses and jockeys go down to the starting gate, and a few yards from me, there were two or three of the bookies' henchmen. One of the jockeys, and a noted clever twister, came slowly cantering by these men, I overheard them say to him, "Cert to win today, B." He replied, "Not if the bloody reins don't break." The henchmen went back to the bookies ring like greased lightning. That was one <u>certain</u> loser.

After one of the races, I lined up in the queue where the bookie was paying out, and just in front of me a woman had handed her ticket to the bookie. He looked at it and said, "Well, Madam, what do you want?" She replied, "Five shillings and my shilling back." The bookie laughed, "But your horse didn't win, Madam, you backed a loser, and lost your money." The woman shouted, "But you told me that I should get five to one." The bookie said gently, "Yes, madam, I know, but I said, also, if your horse won, but it lost." The woman kept shouting, and said she would fetch a policeman and the patient man could not stand it any longer, so he told her, "Madam, fetch a policeman if you like, you're holding the queue up, and they want their winnings, if you don't go I shall have to be very rude, and tell you to bugger off."

Racing is a splendid and exhilarating pastime if you can afford it, and strong-willed enough to keep control of yourself. Once the germ, shall we say, gets well into your blood, you are apt to go beyond your income, and unless you are one of the lucky few, land yourself and your family in a lot of trouble which sometimes takes a long time to overcome, and get on an even keel again. My advice is have a bet on if you want to, and can afford it, but don't go too heavy, or it will get you down.

To show you what I mean by going to extremes, I will just give you three short true stories.

W. was a clerk in the offices of a local factory. He had also got a good connection as a bookie's runner, which made a good addition to his wages. On Derby Day, when the daily paper came on the streets with the results, W. went out and got one. When he got back into the office, he looked pale and worried, had a look at the paper, and then rushed off to the lavatory; when he came back, he had another look at the paper, and off he rushed again. After a time he came back, one of his pals said, "What's the matter, W., you do look ill." W. replied, "Ill, I'll say that I am ill, I had a bet given to me, £5 each-way on that bloody outsider, Blenheim, it's won at 20 to 1 and I stuck to the bet, now what am I going to do?" I don't know what he did, but he would certainly get into a lot of trouble with the punter, and the bookmaker who was employing him.

A. was another bookmaker's runner, he had worked up a large connection, which had brought in a good weekly income for several years. He had bought a lovely house, and fitted it up with modern appliances, and really good furniture. Some of his clients were betting in fairly large sums, which made his commission very good. He got too ambitious, or shall we say greedy, started up on his own account as the bookmaker. Instead of running his book with the small punters, and laying off some portion of the big money so as to cover some of the risk, he tried to keep it all. He lasted out alright for two or three months, and then came several weeks when the punters had a run of luck, couldn't do anything wrong, and hit him hard and heavy. To cover his liabilities, he had to sell his house and furniture and it affected his health. He went away from the district, and I never heard what he was doing, or whether he had pulled round again.

G. was another chap that I knew. He was a good hard-working chap, married, with a large family. He ran a greengrocery round in the daytime, and had a good evening newspaper round. He was a punter in a small way, and like all racing and football betting enthusiasts, had dreams of hitting the jackpot, and making big money. During the middle of one Flat Racing season, his grandmother died, and left G. just over £400, and it just turned his head. He didn't know the inside business of bookmaking, but he started up in a small way. Gordon Richards was having a very successful season, and the punters 'bumped' G. right and left, and he lost £300. This did not teach him his lesson, so he started with fixed odds football tickets, the first three weeks of the season were disastrous, and he lost the remainder of his £400 legacy. Poor old G., he thought he knew it all but he didn't.

Chapter 25

The months rolled on and we were still doing fairly good business, my family was growing up, and Tommy was beginning to be very useful at home, he was also doing well at school. My Little Lady was looking very well and we were very happy and enjoying life to the full. Mabel also enjoyed living with us, she was very attractive and always had plenty of admirers who wanted to take her out on her day off.

Mabel, mid 1920s

My father-in-law 'passed on' after being ill for some weeks. I think the worry of what he had been through, while he was at the pub had seriously affected his health, because he was not an old man, and always fairly active.

The policy of the Tory Government, and foreign competition, was gradually making things worse for the working population and the numbers on short time and on the dole, increased every month. The cinemas were full up in the very cheap seats, but the pubs, especially those in the town centres, were beginning to feel the pinch in the midweek.

One mid-week morning, when the Council Elections were about to take place, I was in the bar, and one of the local Magistrates came in. He was an ex-farmer, black whiskered, tight fisted, the sort of man that would have jailed a man if he caught him looking over his gate, and he wouldn't give a blind man a light. He walked up to the bar, didn't order a drink, and said, "Good Morning, Mr. Clarke, I guess you know what I have called in for ?" I replied, "I have got a good idea, Mr. -, you are after my vote in the coming elections." "That's right, Mr. Clarke, of course we can rely on your vote, and your influence as well." I replied, "What makes you think that, Mr. -?" He said, "Well, it's only common sense, we all know, and you as a businessman should know, that the Conservative Party is always out to do its best for the country, and the business people as well."

I looked straight at him, and said, "The Coal-Owners and the Conservative Party threw my Dad onto the scrapheap after more than sixty years of good service, with the paltry sum of ten shillings a week. Also, I was crippled for life, and received the paltry sum of one hundred pounds, look around at the empty seats in here, go and have a look at the ever-increasing numbers in the dole queues, and you say Toryism is good for business. I have never voted for a Conservative in my life, and I shall never do so." He said, "I can see I am wasting my time, it's no use me talking to you, good day." As he was opening the door to go out, I told him, "Mr. -, this is the only time you've been in to see me, <u>well</u>, you needn't come in here again, <u>good day</u>."

The trade unions were gradually building up their strength and also their reserves, but the movement was not 100% strong, which gave the employers more scope in their efforts to break up different sections in the country, and so cut wages and prevent conditions being altered and improved in many industries. The miners, the dockers, the railwaymen, transport workers, and the engineering workers were all very dissatisfied and discontented with the wage cuts, and this led to the Miners Strike in 1926, when the railwaymen came out in sympathy, and caused almost a complete standstill in the country. But the effort 'fizzled out', and the miners went back to work, on the same terms, and in some cases, worse.

The Labour Party had a short time in power in 1924 with Ramsay MacDonald as Prime Minister, but their majority in the House depended on the Liberals backing them up, and they didn't last long. One big mistake they made was to make Philip Snowden Chancellor of the Exchequer. This austere, unimaginative, cold mathematician, in his first Budget, put a penny on a pint of beer, which got the working man's back up straight away and lost the Labour Party thousands of votes at the next election. His policy was the wrong one to get the popular vote.

In 1926 we received word from the Burton Brewery Company that the brewery and all their licensed houses had been taken over by Ind, Coope and Company, and that all payments were to be made to their representative. This was a big setback to our trade, as the quality of the draught beers and ales was not up to the standard of the B.B. Company. Our outdoor trade began to decline, and mid-week trade fell off as well. It was only the busy weekend business that kept us going, and our bank balance began to get into the red, and the charges made it worse.

I kept the account owing to the B.B. Company separate, and wrote to Ind, Coope, and Company informing them that owing to the trade falling off, and also to the slump in the country, I could only pay the current accounts for the goods they were supplying, and that the amount outstanding to the B.B. Company would have to wait until times got better, and trade improved.

Chapter 26

Time rolled on, and the employment situation and problem was getting worse instead of better. Tommy left the Grammar School much earlier than I had intended, and went to a temporary job at a Coventry engineering factory, until I got him fixed up as an apprentice to the Gas Engineering Department at Nuneaton Gas Works.

In the summer of 1926, my Little Lady told me that we were going to have another baby, so as the winter months came along Tommy had to get used to serving behind the bar in order to relieve my wife during busy times.

On February 27th, 1927, my youngest daughter, Audrey, was born nearly nine years after the birth of Mollie. She was a lovely child, but very small[30]. It was very late when we went to bed, we had not been there long when my wife asked me to get up and send for the midwife as she felt ill. I sent for Alec, and asked him to go as fast as he could on the cycle, and bring the midwife as soon as she could possibly come and off he went like a shot.

It was a dark, stormy night, and absolutely raining in bucketfuls, when Alec came back with the midwife, he was soaked through to the skin. I gave him a good stiff glass of rum, and then told him to go home and get to bed. I filled a pint bottle with old ale, also a small bottle with rum, and told him to have the ale hot with the rum in it when he was in bed. I also told him to have a day's rest away from work, and that I would pay him for it. Good old Alec, he was a proper hero that night.

---

[30] *George himself was only a few inches above 5 feet tall, so his continuous references to Gertie as his Little Lady have more than a hint of irony. Norah and Audrey were both under 4'11" (1.47m), and Mollie not much taller.*

The Wedding of Mabel Brooks to Joseph Beasley, taken in the garden of The King William, November 2nd 1926.

Back row: Percy Brooks, Levi Brooks, Fred Brooks, George Burchnall (Groom's brother in law)

Standing: Eadie Gray, George Clarke, Gertie Clarke carrying baby Audrey, Mabel Daulman, Florence Brooks, Charlotte Brooks, Emily Brooks, Elsie Brooks, Lizzie Wilson, Elsie Burchnall (Groom's sister with baby David)

Seated: Mrs Ensor, Mrs Beasley, Norah Clarke, Ethel Beasley Joseph Beasley (groom)[31], Mabel Brooks (bride), Beth King, Mollie Clarke, Eliza Brooks, Betty Brooks

On ground: Freddie Brooks (son of Fred), Jackie Wilson, Herbert Wilson

---

[31] *Joe left school at the age of 11.*

My wife and the baby went on very well during the first week, but my Little Lady had a relapse, and it was only by the Doctor's skill, combined with good nursing, that kept her going and after a few weeks she regained her health, and was her old self again. Mabel was a good help to us at this period, she stuck to her work and also looked after my wife and children, which left me free to look after the pub and the business.

Audrey in 1928

In 1928, we had a reminder from the brewery company that nothing had been done to reduce the amount outstanding on the company old account, and this was followed by a visit from the manager who was in charge of all the licensed houses, owned or leased by the company, in our, and the surrounding districts. He was an ex-Army officer, very keen, brusque, and overbearing. He was new to the business and lacked any sympathy for anyone who was unable to come up to his expected ideas as to how accounts should be met, and could not understand that we had to live as well as pay the standing charges.

We had a rather long talk together, and I pointed out to him the improvements that I had made to the pub, yard and garden. This did not cut much ice with him, his main purpose was the financial side of the business. He said that the amount of trade we were doing, ought to cover all standing charges, provide a good living wage, and still leave a surplus, which could be used to reduce the Burton Brewery Company old account.

I told him that the margin of profit on the present turnover was not enough to justify this, that we had to pay a pianist at weekends to attract custom, nor could we charge extra on the smoke room trade, or the customers would not come in there, and finally, that we ought to have some allowance towards the rates, and the coal used in the winter time. When he left me, he said that he would consider the matter over and let me know later.

I told my Little Lady some of the details, but not too much, as I did not want to worry her. Many times during our happy married life, she got on my 'track', because I did not let her know when things were not going too well, but I knew that I could bear the burden and face up to any situation without worrying her, she had enough to do to cope with the household duties, and look after the children as well.

Some weeks later, I received a letter from the Brewery company, asking us to go to Burton on Trent, to talk matters over with the General Manager. My wife and I went to the company's offices, and met the Manager, who had the House Manager with him. We sat down together and the interview began, after a few friendly words. The General Manager said that in the report he had received, he was quite satisfied with the way in which we conducted the business, but there was the B.B. Company old outstanding account which was troubling them, and we must make an effort to reduce this in some way.

I told them that it was not possible in our present circumstances to make any offer, and that in any case, we did not owe any money to them other than the current account, the money was owing to the B.B. Company which was now extinct. This shook both of them for a moment or two, then the Manager said that they had taken over the brewery, licensed houses, and debts as well.

I asked him how much they had paid for our outstanding account, and he replied that it was not my business to ask that question. I told him that it was not my intention to try and pay them in full for something which most likely they had obtained for a mere song. Both of them looked at my wife and me, not to each other, and asked me if I would hand over my valuation of security and accept the position of Manager, instead of being the tenant, but on a good weekly wage.

This was not so bad, until I asked them about security of tenure, and they said the usual terms, a months notice on either side. I told them that I could not accept such a settlement. When they had got my valuation they could give me a months notice, or a months wages, and chuck me out whenever they liked. They both said that this was not likely to happen, muttered together again for a minute or two, and then made another proposal.

This was to the effect, that if I would give three months notice, and also say that I was willing to transfer my Licence, the company would cancel all the old amount that was owing to the B.B. Company, and that all the balance, when the current account was settled from the valuation, would be handed over to me. This was more to my liking, and we signed a temporary agreement, which was properly fixed up, by a stamped agreement later on. The Manager gave us two pounds to cover expenses, so we had lunch and returned home.

When we talked the matter over, my wife said, "Well, George, you have done it again, what are we going to do now, and where do we go from here?" I told her not to worry, that was my job, but in any case, it was impossible to carry on at the pub, trade was going from bad to worse, and it looked black for everybody, owing to the unemployment situation in the country. Some few weeks later, I heard a rumour that the tenant of the shop belonging to me was thinking of leaving the district, so I went to have a talk with him. He told me that he was leaving, also that he had received a good offer for the business and had accepted it. I said, "Now, let's get down to business. This is my property, and it is not in your power to transfer the business to another tenant without my permission, which I shall not give. I require the house for myself and the family, so let us come to terms over the fixtures, etc." After a good deal of argument I settled up with him, and paid £20 for the fixtures and loss of business. This left the premises clear, and in my spare time I started to give the old house a thorough cleanup, assisted by my wife's sister, Lizzie, who was an expert at paper-hanging, and the result was well worth the labour and time.

The end of June 1928 was when our notice expired at the pub, and the valuation took place on the day we were leaving. Previous to this the House Manager called again, to check up on the fixtures, etc. Before he left, I asked him to have a look around the back yard and the garden, and said, "How much are you prepared to pay for these improvements, because it was an ash-tip when we came here." He laughed and replied, "Oh, we can't pay you anything for such as that, you did it for your own pleasure." I told him that if he did not pay, I should pull all the lot down, and chop all the rose trees and shrubs to bits. This put the breeze up, and after a heated argument, he agreed to allow me £50. It was only by sticking up for my rights, and also for myself and family, that I finished well on the right side, with a decent amount of money to start on our new venture.

Lizzie Brooks, expert decorator

The next few years proved that I was correct about the general outlook. Numbers of licensees had to give up, many of them were nearly broke. The young couple who followed us as tenants had to leave the pub after about four years, they had lost all their capital, and were in debt into the bargain.

Chapter 27

As soon as we had settled into our new abode, we stripped all the walls in the shop, gave them all a good wash down and then a good coat of limewash with plenty of carbolic disinfectant mixed in it. When this was dry, we re-papered the walls, and painted all the woodwork, etc. I put a lot of new shelves up, repaired the store cupboards, and had the lighting of the shop changed from gas to electricity.

**Norah, Audrey, and Mollie
outside the shop in Coton Road, Summer 1930**

Then we stocked the place with cigarettes, groceries, tinned goods, biscuits, and sweets of all kinds. Later we introduced fruit and greengrocery. We also tried to get a connection for pork, sausages, and made up goods, but the shortage of money spoilt the prospects for these lines.

The margin of profit was too small, and as they soon went wrong if they were not cleared daily, it meant a dead loss.

Trade was fairly good, and it would have been a really good venture if there had been more money about, and the danger of shady customers. Some of these were always on the prowl, ready to tell the tale, get as much as they could on credit and then try somewhere else on the same game, until no one would trust them.

Others who were very straightforward, had very little to spend in the week time, and I supplied several families with goods for their dinner, which amounted to about sevenpence. Corned beef ¼lb = 2d, potatoes 2lbs = 2½d, onions 1lb = 1½d. Their other meals were mainly bread, with either butter, margarine, lard, or cheese.

Some days we were almost over-run by commercial travellers, who were all over the country and thousands tried to push all kinds of different commodities on to shop-keepers, some of which took months to clear, or perhaps never were cleared. They almost got on their knees and begged for a small order, most of them were on a commission only agreement, they soon got fed up, and we never saw them again.

In addition to these, the national newspapers were on the war-path, trying to increase their circulation. Their canvassers were proper pests, trying to get people to change from one paper to another.

The big cigarette firms were on the same stunt, with coupon and gift schemes, cigarette cards, so that all the time small shops were open, there was a traveller in every hour or less.

The advertising firms who specialise in the window stick-on banners and signs were also a nuisance, some of them would not take a polite no to their appeals, and had to be told their name with knobs on before they would go.

However after a few weeks experience, we found out what would sell, and how to deal with the commercial travellers who were only out to get as much commission as possible, and leave you with junk on your shelves. There was no trouble with tea and coffee firms such as Lyons and Brooke Bonds, they came round with their vans which were nothing more than travelling shops. Goods were supplied to the shops in any quantity, but the terms were cash down, no credit was allowed at all. Their representative told me that they were liable to be pulled up at any time by the District Inspector, who would check their stock and cash, and if they did not balance, they were in for a lot of trouble. Our regular wholesalers were very good and helpful, they did not try to overstock us with goods that would not sell well. The margin of profit was very small on some of the goods, and not very big on the others.

To help the weekly income, I worked as a collector and canvasser for a local check firm, which really was another description for money lending. For every pound cheque issued, the customer had to pay twenty-one shillings, and the check could only be exchanged for goods at shops on the firm's list, these shopkeepers were charged four shillings in the pound to cover the cost of canvassing and collecting.

The check firm settled up with the shopkeepers every month, and naturally the extra was passed on, and paid for by the check customer. This was a poor prospect so after a few weeks, I packed this up, it wasn't worth the time and trouble.

One night looking down the Situations Vacant in the local paper, I saw that a Leamington Brewery wanted a local representative. I made an application and was asked to go for an interview the following week. When I reached Leamington on the appointed day, there was about a mile to walk, and when I reach the brewery I asked the man in

175

charge of the office to let Mr. Thornley know that I had come for the interview. He said, "I am very sorry, but your journey is in vain, Mr. Thornley died suddenly this morning, so we shall have to write to you later, when his successor is appointed."

A few weeks later, after another interview, I was given the post of Representative. My job was to canvass from house to house the bottled beer, ale, stout, cider, and also collect the money. The brewery manager wanted me to accept commission only, but only after a good deal of discussion, he agreed to pay ten shillings per week, plus 10% commission on all sales.

This position, in ordinary times, would have been quite a good job, but again the shortage of money and the ever-increasing unemployment, spoilt the prospects. Quite a large number of people would have been customers, but they could not afford to buy beer, etc., the money was required for cost of living and household necessities. As it was, I worked up quite a decent round, which brought a few extra shillings in to help keep us going in a quiet way.

Some few months after, I had a visit from the Income Tax Collector, and he wanted the sum of 15 shillings, which he said was owing from the last year at the pub. I told him that the last two years there had been a dead loss, that I was out of work and unable to get any, and as I had been self-employed it was not possible for me to sign on at the Labour Exchange, and get the dole. I told him that he could cancel it out as I did not intend to pay, so off he went, very annoyed.

My wife told me that he had called in two or three times after this episode, she said, "Pay him, George, you will only get into some more trouble if you don't, he told me so." I replied, "Not likely, he won't get anything off me, they would have your last drop of blood."

176

A week later, he came into the shop in the early part of the morning, and I wasn't in a very pleasant mood just at that moment. He said, "Good Morning, Mr. Clarke, I guess you know what I have come after, so pay up, there's a good chap, and I can clear my books." I looked at him, and replied, "I told you my intentions the last time I saw you, and still you keep coming, well, there's the kitchen table, put that on your bloody hump and take it with you, that will clear the fifteen bob." He went out of the shop like a shot, and never called again, that cleared the account.

My Little Lady said, "Oh, our George, you should not have treated him like that, you'll get yourself into trouble one of these days." I replied, "Don't worry yourself, old girl, I knew what I was doing, he wants to round up those who owe quids, not somebody who only owes a few bob."

One Thursday afternoon (it was closing day for all the big shops) a man opened the shop door, came just inside, and said, "Hello, Mr. Clarke, you know me, don't you, I often used to come in your pub." I replied, "Yes, I've seen you once or twice, what can I do for you?" He asked me if I would let him have two ounces of "twist" until Friday night, as his wife had forgotten to get him any. I asked him where he bought his tobacco from every week, and he said that his wife got it from the Co-op, but they were closed. "Well," I replied, "you bugger off round the Co-op and get some, you're not going to twist me."

Both at the pub and the shop, some folks thought us public benefactors, or good Samaritans, we were their father confessors in all their trials and troubles, and God knows they had plenty at that time, many of them were always very hard up, and didn't know what to do for the best from week to week.

Chapter 28

My brother, Sidney, was in clover at this period, his father-in-law, Mr. S. Smith, had been rolling the money in, from the old Picture Palace in Victoria Street, and had built the new Palace Cinema, which now stands in Queens Road.[32] Sid was manager for his father-in-law, and as he was a very good electrical engineer, this experience came in very useful.

One day when I had been talking to him about the unemployment problem, explaining my position and how hard it was to get a suitable job, owing to my crippled right leg, he said that he would have a talk with Mr. Smith, and see if they could fix me up. Later on I went to see the old man, and he told me that I could have a job helping Sid, and looking after things when he or Sid were away. He said that he could not pay me a big wage, but at least it would tide me over for a time, and my Unemployment and Insurance (Health) Card would be stamped, and so put me in benefit. ﹏

I started to work at the cinema, three hours in the afternoons, five hours in the evenings, so that I was able to look after the shop in the mornings, and also carry on with the canvassing and collecting from the brewery company.

It is surprising how easy some work, or business, looks to the person or persons on the outside. It is only when they get inside that they realise how little they do know, and what a lot there is to learn. British films at this time

---

[32] *The building was erected in 1889 on the corner of Victoria Street and Queens Road, as The Palace Gardens Working Men's Club. The new Palace Cinema was built on what had been the garden, and opened in December 1928, and seated 990 people: the last silent film was shown there on 11th-13th December 1930. After the new Palace was built the old one was converted into a roller skating rink, and then in 1931 into a ballroom.*

were not up to the standard of the Americans, although they were making good progress. Geaumont British were just beginning to make headway, one of two of their feature films were really good, though most of the others could not compare with Hollywood productions, for action, thrills, interest and up-to-date subjects.

The Block system of booking films was just beginning to be introduced, this was as follows. If the cinema owner or manager wanted to book two and or three really good feature films which would be sure money-spinners, he had to take several second raters as well, in order to obtain the top liners. Also, if the full renters knew they had got a real money-spinner, it was only distributed on sharing terms, and the renters usually wanted the lion's share.

A cinema manager has to be, or ought to be, well spoken, well-dressed, blessed with a good personality, charming manners, tact, and have enough ability to deal with any situation. He is expected to be a good publicity expert, good staff controller, and tireless in his efforts to make the cinema clean, warm, and comfortable for all its patrons, so the business keeps good. In addition he ought to (and usually does) know quite a lot about electrical engineering and lighting, maintenance and upkeep of seating, upholstery, and the practice and general routine of the projecting room, including up-keep.

During the year I was employed at the cinema, I met and talked to many of the people engaged in the film industry, some of them would always remain and be content to be in the same old ruts, but one at two of them were real live wires, and in later years were promoted to executive positions by the large film distributing and renting companies.

One in particular was a good-looking man in his thirties, well built, about 6'3" in height, full of vim and the joy of living. He came about every two or three months, and each time he came, he had got a fresh dame, and every other visit or so, a new car. I heard later on that he was promoted and was a big shot in the Metro-Goldwyn-Mayer Corporation.

When these travellers came, they were like leeches, and hung on to Sid, sometimes for hours, until they had obtained an order. When he thought someone was coming, who we did not want to meet, I had to tell them he was out.

A few weeks after I had started to work at the cinema, I noticed how wet weather made a lot of difference to the takings, especially to the second evening performance, when people were waiting and queuing up. After looking round and weighing things up, I asked Mr. Smith to have a look round with me, and pointed out how much room there was to spare in the yard, and all round the building, and suggested to him that if a covered shelter, three or four yards wide was fixed up along the side and into the adjoining street, there would be enough room to keep enough people dry, which would fill all the ground floor, a privilege which was not possible at any of the other cinemas.

He said that it was a really good suggestion, had the shelters made straightaway, and the people showed their appreciation, there was always a full house for the late performance, especially when the weather was very bad.

The 'talkies' were just beginning to become popular, though the reproduction of the human voice was very poor at first, and some of the stars who had swept the boards in the silent films needed expert advice and tuition. Their voices and speech needed cultivation, they grated and sent shivers up your back.

A large number of our actors and actresses came into their own, some of them had always seemed stiff and awkward in the silent films, but in the talkies, their diction and elocution sounded lovely: compared with the Hollywood accents they seemed to lose all their stiffness and were more natural.

One actor whom I noticed in particular, was Stuart Roma. In all the silent films, he had been as stiff as a poker then, what a difference, in the talkies, he was the perfect English gentleman, both in his manners, action, and speech.

The first talkie shown in Nuneaton, starred Al Jolson singing 'Sunny Boy', and did the women enjoy it? I'll say they did, they cried their eyes out, some of them went two or three times.

Mr. Smith often came and had a quiet talk to me, and always asked me on the Monday nights when I had seen the programme through, what I thought of it, and whether it would be successful, draw the people in, and so ensure a good week. I always told him what I thought and he valued my opinion. I have got enough experience and intuition to know what the public wanted and liked.

The old man lived long enough to see the talkies installed at the Palace, but several months later his health began to fail, gradually got worse, and had to stay in bed. After about six months, he 'passed on', and that was the end of a 'grand old man'.

My brother Sid and his wife (the old man's daughter) were now in full control, and they were also running the old Palace as a dance hall. It had been redecorated, a new floor laid, good lighting, and a refreshment bar installed. They did good business and it was a good paying proposition. The younger generation, who were born just before the First World War, and during it, were growing up and taking advantage of every form of excitement and enjoyment, when they could afford it.

Chapter 29

The trade at the shop was very steady, but we kept pulling through, and at least we always lived well, even if there wasn't much money to throw about.

Audrey with Dinah the family dog, early 1930s

A traveller came into the shop one day, he was rather brusque and overbearing, but he had a good line in a cheap carbolic scrubbing soap, so I gave him a small order. It sold very well, so the next time he came I ordered a double quantity, but he sent a very big case, about eight times as much. When the time came round for his next visit, I told my Little Lady to tell him that I would pay him on his next visit, and that we didn't want any more soap for the time being. He called, and my wife said that he was very nasty and demanded money, she said that she would not see him again, nor deal with him.

When he called the next time, I was in, I put the account on the counter, and the money, told him to settle it, and give me the receipt. He did so, smiled, then said, "I'm going to send you another case, and we have another good line I will send you at the same time." I replied, "You're not going to send me anything, if I want anything, I order it. When you learn how to treat a lady, you will do better business, we don't want any more of your soap, nor do we want to see you again." He picked up his bag, and went like a shot.

Another traveller, he represented one of the biggest concerns in the canned food industry in the country, who were putting a new line of theirs on the market. I didn't want any, but his sales talk and persuasion eventually succeeded, and I ordered a small quantity. The goods came two or three weeks later, and I had only just put the goods on show, when in walked the traveller, he smiled, and said, "Good Morning, Mr. Clarke, I see that the goods have come, how are they selling?" I replied, "They have only just come, so I can't tell you." He mentioned the account, and I told him to call next time, when I cleared some of the stock. The same week, about two days after his call, I received a County Court order to pay the amount of the account, plus costs amounting to about eight shillings. I ignored this, and waited until his Lordship called again.

He was all dressed up like a city businessman, black jacket, striped trousers, bowler hat, and tightly rolled

183

umbrella and came in full of beans. "Good Morning, Mr. Clarke, now what can I do for you?" "Well," I replied, "the first thing you can do is to settle this account, here's your money." "But what about the costs of the County Court order ?" he said, "You will have to pay them." I told him straight and to the point, "You pushed the goods on to me, wanted payment for them before I had sold any, and then had the audacity to send the C.C. order, you settle that account *at once*, and you, or your firm can pay the costs, if you don't, I shall explain the facts of the case to the C.C. judge, and make an offer of sixpence per week, which he will accept."

He stamped and receipted the account, picked the money up, and went out of the shop not so full of the joy of life as he was when he came in. I saw him go by several times afterwards, but he always walked on the other side of the road. I mentioned this affair to one of my regular wholesaler's traveller, he laughed, and said I had done quite right, and told me about an incident in his early career on the road.

A very good customer of his kept a grocery and provision shop in an outlying village. She was doing very well, and had been one of his firm's best customers for a very long period. Several months after he had been on the round, this old lady missed paying her account two calls in succession, but ordered her usual goods, and this made him get a bit anxious. When he made his next call, he mentioned the account and the old lady looked at him, smiled, and said, "So you don't trust me, young man, I was just testing you; for the past thirty years I have been one of your firm's best customers, never owing them a penny, you ought to have known that, but you're too young and impulsive, you will learn as you grow older." Then she went into the room behind the shop, and came back again with a big bucket full of coppers. She said, "Now, count that up, you can settle the account and never ask me again, or I shall finish with the firm altogether."

He told me that it taught him a lesson, which he never forgot, it made him very tactful when dealing with fresh people and their accounts.

Another traveller, a nice old man, was in the salt and vinegar trade. He told me that he had done very well in his younger days, and had saved about two thousand pounds towards the time when he wanted to steady down, or retire. He lived at Birmingham. One of his friends was a partner in a flourishing iron bedstead manufacturing firm, and persuaded the old man to invest all his money in this concern. After two or three years, the iron bedsteads went off the market, wooden ones were all the rage, and the firm in which he had invested his capital went into liquidation, so that nearly all his savings were gone, and the old man had started back on the 'trail' again.

We had a fishmonger who supplied us with fish once or twice a week. He was a good sort, full of fun, and we always got on well with him. One day when he called, I noticed that he had got the thumb on his right hand very heavily bandaged, and I asked him what he had done. He said, "You know that I am left-handed, I was chopping some fish with my big knife, it was very icy and slipped, and I chopped my thumb." I replied, "You were very lucky, Burt, you might have chopped it off altogether." He laughed and said, "It's a really good job that I didn't, that thumb has earned me pounds, I've weighed it thousands of times."

One day there was a small fire in one of the bedrooms of one of the four cottages belonging to me. It smoked the walls badly and burnt the paint off the window frame. I made a claim for five pounds from the Fire Insurance Company to cover the damage. The Inspector and a local builder came and inspected it, but did not call in to see me, although our house was only at the bottom of the yard. A workman came next day, distempered the walls, and painted the window frame.

I received a cheque for five pounds from the Insurance company the next week, and by the same post, there came a bill from the builder, for five pounds for work done, but no details. I wrote to the builder, and asked for a detailed statement, as I was not satisfied that five pounds worth of work had been done. He called in to see me, and said that he had put in an estimate for the amount in question, which they had accepted, and it was up to me to settle the account. I told him to send me a detailed statement of the work done, then I would pay him. He refused to do this, and went out very annoyed.

Two or three days after, the Insurance Inspector came to see me. He was a very big man over six feet tall, broad shouldered, and rather brusque in his manners, he thought he could put the breeze up me, as I'm only just over five feet. He said, "Now, Mr. Clarke, we sent you the cheque to cover the amount of your claim, and it is up to you to pay Mr. -, the builder, who estimated and completed the work for us." I told them that when I received a detailed statement, the account would be settled. He argued a bit, and then went.

A week went by, and into the shop he came again, looking very stern, and said, "Now, Mr. Clarke, you must settle the account, or you'll get yourself into a lot of trouble. We sent you the cheque to cover the cost of the estimate, and you must pay Mr. -, the builder." I looked at him, and said, "Who paid the Fire Insurance Premium, did you pay it? Did Mr. -, the builder, pay it? Or did I pay it?" He replied, "Why, of course, you paid it." So I told him straight, "Well, now we know, and if there's any bunce out of this deal, Mr. - is not going to get it, nor you. I will pay Mr. - for what he has done when he sends me a detailed statement, and the balance belongs to me." Off he went, and I never heard any more of the affair. The Insurance company must have paid the builder, and I had five pounds for nothing. The Inspector and the builder thought that there would be an easy four pounds to split between them.

This just shows what rackets are going on all the time, and it pays everyone to use their brains and common sense when making a business deal. Some of these business experts would pinch the milk out of your tea.

The unemployment question was still a big problem, more than two million on the dole, and thousands more who were not able to draw this meagre pittance, people who had been self-employed, or working at some job which did not cover unemployment or health-insurance. The Government did not seem to have any idea how to deal with the problem, nor did they seem to care, with the result that the Labour Party got into power again, with a small majority. The same old gang formed the Government, Ramsay MacDonald, Philip Snowden, Jimmy Thomas, and company, they were too weak and spineless to do anything drastic, and in addition there was the biggest slump in the United States that had ever been known, so they did not last long.

Chapter 30

Our children were growing up now. Tommy was doing well at the Gas Company's Offices and Works, though as he was an apprentice his wage was very poor, but he was not over-reaching, and did not expect more than we could afford for clothes and spending money. He was also attending technical classes which took up a lot of his spare time.

Mollie, 1930

Norah was at work as an assistant in a local boot and shoe shop, where she worked hard for four shillings a week, and Mollie was still at school. They were both very nice girls, well spoken, nice dispositions, good appearance and well mannered. Audrey was the pet lamb of the family, she was a pretty little girl, her mother's (and mine) pride and joy, and all of us made a rare fuss of her, she was able to get her own way in most things.

Norah at Nuneaton Swimming Baths, 1932

Tommy was always full of life and fun, and sometimes as I was in the shop going through the book, or checking up, he would walk quietly into the shop in his stockinged feet, come right behind me and say, "Now, what do you reckon you're doing," usually it made me jump nearly out of my skin, then off he would walk, laughing his sides sore. I had always taught him to stand up for himself, speak the truth, and never to be afraid of anyone. One day at work, the manager had questioned Tommy about some work, and he answered and explained what he had done and asked, was that right? The manager, who was very fiery and hot-tempered, told him "No, it was all wrong, it ought to have been done in such and such a way." Tommy stuck to his guns, and said that he'd done the work the same way that he had been taught by the company's engineers, and he thought that it was correct and quite all right. This got the manager's temper up, and he told poor Tommy his name with knobs on, and said, "I know best."

The lad was rather upset when he came home for dinner, and told me what had happened. I said, "Never mind, Tom, always stick to your opinion, when you are confident that you are right, but don't be afraid to admit it when you are wrong." He replied, "Righto, Dad, I knew you would back me up." When I saw him later on that night, he was all teeth and smiles, he told me that the 'old man' had sent for him, and then told him that he was sorry for his outburst, the work had been done quite correctly, and that he was not to worry himself.

One holiday time, I think it was Whitsuntide, Tommy said to me, "How are you fixed, Dad, I could do with a new suit. I feel very shabby when I go out at weekends." I replied, "Not very well at the moment, Tom, I'm afraid you'll have to wait a bit longer." He said, "Have you got a good horse today? I see that you are sorting them out." There was a horse named Verdant Green, entered at Wolverhampton Races, which I fancied. I told him, and he gave me two shillings each way to put on it. It won at 20 to 1, which made him 54 shillings to come back. Tommy got his new suit.

Sometimes at supper time, when we had got time to talk about different subjects, I got going on one of my favourite subjects, Tom would take the opposite view on purpose to get my hair off. Once, when he had tormented me a bit too much, there was half a loaf of bread on the table and I picked it up and threw it at him. He dodged it, and said, "Sorry, Dad, better luck next time." Whenever we got debating after that, if I got a bit hot under the collar, he would laugh and say, "Wait a minute Dad, I'll go and fetch the loaf."

Tommy with girlfriend, 1930

When he was 21, he applied for a job at the Coventry Gas Corporation, one of the most up-to-date concerns in the country. He was successful and became a fully qualified Gas fitter, his wages were increased by a considerable amount, and it gave him every chance to gain the valuable practical experience that he needed. The first problem that he came up against was the time spent on the different jobs. The trade union was very strong, and their opinions were very strong on the time taken to complete the different jobs. Tom didn't know for some time how long he was supposed to take, or whether he was completing the job fast enough for the company. He asked me for my opinion, I told him to be sure and make a good, sound job of everything which he was sent to do, and that if he did it too quickly the union men would advise him, and on the other hand, if it had taken too long, the company's Inspector would soon tell him.

After a week or two, he got well into his stride, and told me that there was always plenty of time allowed for different work, and a lot of spare time to cover awkward jobs in time. He attended Coventry Technical College, where he made good progress, so what with his work, his classes, and travelling to and from Coventry, his time was fully occupied from week to week. He was a big help to my wife, as he increased the amount towards the household expenses considerably, and this gave her a bit more to spend on her household needs.

I always got up first in the mornings, and got Tom's breakfast ready for him. He knew he'd get my hair off very easily, and sometimes he would say, "Was the water boiling when you made this tea?" Or "Did you sort out one of the oldest eggs in the shop for me, this one doesn't smell too good." I usually told him to get the bugger down, and not waste time, or he would miss his train.

After he had been working at Coventry about two years, he bought a second-hand motor-cycle, a big, clumsy, heavy thing, but he must have found plenty of fun and interest in it. He always got it going, and rode to and from Coventry, in addition to using it to get from place to place when at work.

It took him quite a long time some mornings to get it to start up, and one morning it conked out on his way to work. He was adjusting it and trying to get it going again, and a man stood looking on for several minutes. Eventually he said, "What's up, pal, won't she go?" Tom, who like me, was a bit short- tempered, looked up and replied, "What the hell do you think is up, do you think I am cleaning the bugger?"

Tommy Clarke aged 21

He was now doing well at work, the Sales Manager for Coventry Gas Company had taken a great deal of interest in him, made him his assistant, and pushed him along as much as he could.

My Dad 'passed on' at the ripe old age of 81, there was nothing physically wrong with him, he just faded out. For all his faults in his younger days, he was a grand old man, and altered his ways a lot in his old age.

Tommy Clarke on his motor-cycle

I used to feel sorry for him sometimes, it was such a big heavy machine, and it must have mauled him at times, but he would never admit it. After some months he got rid of it in part exchange for a much smaller two-stroke, which was much easier to handle and control. Both his mother and I did not like the idea of him riding a motor-cycle, but youth will be served, and they cannot see any danger. We begged him to sell it and buy a small second-hand car, but he wouldn't agree, so all we could do was to tell him to be careful, take care of himself, and hope for the best.[33]

---

[33] *There is a family story that Tom took Norah on the bike to see their Auntie Mabel and Uncle Joe Beasley on their smallholding on Nutts Lane, near Hinckley. Joe was very wary of motorcycles, because when he was in his teens, a motorcycle had run into the back of his cart, causing the horse to bolt, and Joe had fallen off, badly breaking his left arm and shoulder. It never mended properly: his arm was wired to his shoulder blade, and he could never afterwards raise it above chest height (in his wedding photograph his suit was built up to mask it). As Tom arrived, Joe is reported as saying "...that bike'll be the death of you, young Tommy."*

Chapter 31

Time rolled on, Mollie had now left school, and was employed as a shop assistant. This brought a little more into my Little Lady's household fund, and it looked as if we were going to experience some smoother going for a change, but it was not to be. My wife and I had the most severe blow of our lives. It was a terrible shock to both of us, and also to the children.

Coming home from work on his motorcycle, Tommy collided with a motor van, was thrown off his cycle onto the curb stone, and died instantly from a fractured skull. We never got to know the full details as to how it happened, there were no people about, and no one witnessed the accident.

The van driver gave his own version of the affair at the inquest, and said that he was not to blame in any way, but I did not believe him. Tom was such a careful driver, and if he could take care of himself in a busy place like Coventry, it was very hard to realise that the van driver was as blameless as he declared he was at the inquest, which took place at Coventry. It happened on a wide stretch of road, the sun was shining, there was no other traffic about, only Tom coming home from Coventry, and the van driver going back to the same place. What made me doubt the van driver more, was the fact that he had not enough courage, or shall we say guts, to come and see me, and explain how the accident really happened.

The verdict at the inquest was accidental death, and so another young life was lost through one of the pests of our own present civilisation, the motorcycle. Thousands of young men have met their death on these accursed machines. I hate the sight of them, but the young men cannot see any danger, and ignore what has been happening year after year, and can do again. The speed keeps increasing, and when anything happens the motorcyclist has no protection.

Newspaper Reports on the accident

ROAD ACCIDENT

Inquest on Nuneaton Motor-Cyclist

"ACCIDENTAL DEATH" VERDICT

The inquest on Sidney Thomas Clarke (22), of 75, Coton Road, Nuneaton, who was killed in a road accident on Monday night, was held at Coventry Police Station last evening by the Coroner (Mr. C. W. Iliffe) and a jury.

George Leonard Clarke, father of deceased, said his son was employed by the Coventry Corporation as a gas engineer, and used a light-weight motor cycle for travelling to and from his work.

Girl-Cyclist's Evidence.

Elsie Mortiboy, of 34, York Buildings, Bulkington Lane, Bedworth, said she was cycling home from work when the motor-cyclist passed her at a moderate speed, and within a few yards collided with an oncoming lorry, which appeared to be driven well on the crown of the road in order to pass some road repairs on its near side. The force of the impact caused the front wheel of the motor cycle to fly up into the air and knocked witness from her bicycle, causing injuries to an arm, which had prevented her working since. The road was dry, and the motor cycle did not skid.

"Saw Deceased Hurtling Through the Air."

Mrs. Hester Bates, of 259, Coventry Road, Exhall, who was walking in the roadway, said the lorry passed at a moderate speed. She did not see the motor cycle until her attention was drawn by a terrific bang, and, looking round, she saw deceased hurtling through the air and falling on the road "like a bag of flour." The lorry was on its proper side of the road at the time.

P.C. Lancelot said the motor cycle was in the gutter about five feet from Clarke, who appeared to be dead. The entire front of the machine was smashed. There were several bad potholes near the scene of the accident, and the surface of the road bore brake marks made by the lorry, which extended for fifty feet, finishing up 4ft. 10ins. from its near side kerb. Marks on the lorry indicated that Clarke had struck the side of the driver's cab with his head. There were no marks on the road to indicate the exact point of impact.

Lorry Driver's Statement.

Sidney Wm. Howes, of 16, Mason's Road, Erdington, the driver of the lorry, stated that the latter was a two-tonner fitted with pneumatic tyres, and was proceeding towards Coventry. Witness saw the motor cyclist, and as the rider appeared to be looking back over his shoulder witness sounded his horn when the machine was twenty yards away. The driver did not turn his head towards the lorry, but the cycle appeared to shoot across the road and struck the offside rear wing of the lorry. Prior to the accident witness was driving at about 20 miles an hour, and had just slowed down to pass road repairs and three cyclists. When the accident occurred his speed would be 12 to 15 miles an hour at the time of the impact.

Medical evidence showed that Clarke was dead when taken to the Coventry Hospital the cause of death being a fractured skull and shock arising from extensive multiple injuries all down the right side.

The jury returned a verdict of "Accidental death."

THE LATE MR. S. T. CLARKE.

Accident Victim's Funeral at Coton

The funeral of Mr. Sidney Thomas Clarke, the young motor cyclist, of 73, Coton Road, Nuneaton, who was killed on the Foleshill Road, on Monday night, under circumstances previously reported, took place at Coton Churchyard on Friday afternoon.

The chief mourners were Mr. G. L. Clarke (father) and Mrs. Clarke (mother), and members of the family; Mr. and Mrs. A. E. Clarke (uncle and aunt). Mr. S. Clarke (uncle). and Mrs. E. Brooks (grandmother).

A number of representatives of the Coventry Corporation Gas Department, by whom deceased was employed, including members of staff, attended. Others present included representatives of the Nuneaton Gas Co., at whose works deceased served his apprenticeship.

The bearers were six of deceased's fellow workmen.

The Vicar of Coton (the Rev. J. A. B. Davies) officiated at the service.

Floral tributes were received from the following :—Employees of Coventry City Gas Department; Employees of Nuneaton Gas Company; Mother and Father; Norah, Mollie and Audrey (sisters); Uncle Albert and Aunty Ethel, Dorothy and Jean (Stockingford); Uncle Sid and Aunty Alice (Palace); Cousin Charlie (Palace); Uncle Jack and Aunt Edith and family; Uncle Ernest and Aunty Nell (Walsgrave); Uncle Naoh and Aunty Flo (Coventry); Uncle George and Aunty May ('Black Swan.' Stockingford); Grandma, Aunty Charlotte and Uncle Arthur; Aunty Lizzie, Herbert and Jackie; Uncle Fred, Aunty Pem, Uncle Percy and Aunty Sis; Uncle Sid and Aunty Flo; Albert Gray and Aunty Edith; Mabel and Jack, Bill and Winnie; Joe and Ivy; Winnie and Marjorie; Alice; Mr. and Mrs. Pearson; Mr. and Mrs. Trusslove and family; Mrs. Mortiboy and daughter; Mr. Gater, Jim, Evelyn and Cis; Mr. and Mrs. A. H. Hales; Management and Staff of the New Palace, Queen's Road; Friends and neighbours, Coton Road; Customers, Rose Inn, Coton Road.

The tragedy upset my wife very much, and it was months before she overcame the effects of the shock. As for myself, I did not sleep hardly at all for six months or so. I lay thinking all sorts of things, such as if only I had done so and so at such a time, or, if I hadn't done so and so at such a time, this might not have happened.

It aged me quite a number of years. I felt very bitter, and when I saw ignorant, loudmouthed, empty headed young louts, going through life without a care in the world or any sort or consideration for anyone but themselves, I wondered why a lad like Tom, who had studied and tried to improve himself, should be snatched away before he had really lived.

He had obtained the Diploma and Bronze Medal of the London City and Guilds for Gas Engineering[34], and the Principal of Coventry Technical College informed me that Tom would, no doubt, have gone to greater successes, he was a very clever lad, and his teachers thought a lot of him. I am convinced, myself, that if the terrible accident had not had happened, he would have made good headway, and eventually got a good post on the National Gas Board.

Both my wife and I were very unsettled for a long time and considered whether we ought to make another move to fresh surroundings, but the puzzle was how to find a suitable job, which would enable us to keep on an even keel. The numbers of skilled and able-bodied men who were out of work, or on short time, was increasing every week, so we thought it was the best policy to hold on to what we had got. In any case, it kept us going, if nothing else.

I wrote to several of the brewery companies, and in reply had the offer of several country pubs, but the details of the trade done did not encourage me to apply to any one

---

[34] *The medal is in the family archive.*

199

of them. It looked very much like holding a licence just to pay the rent, and keep the pub open, and also go out to work in order to be able to do so, so we turned that idea down.

Nora and Mollie were now growing up, both of them had obtained better positions, and they were also very helpful to their mother, in addition, they helped with the shop, dressing the window to make it look attractive. One day, Mollie, who was now an assistant in a jeweller's shop, brought home the Peterborough News, her employer had another shop in that town. There was an advert in that paper for a manager to take charge of a public house. I applied, and we were asked to go for an interview.

Mollie and Norah, 1933

So off we went to the brewery at Huntingdon, where we met the General Manager and the Secretary of the company. The terms they offered were very fair, and I think my wife and I create a good impression. They told us that we seem to be the ideal people for the position, and we thought that it was in the bag. They gave us a

200

drink of their best brew, and told the cashier to give us two pounds to cover expenses. Before we went, the manager told us that the name of the pub was the Victoria Inn, where it was situated, and advised us to call and have a good look over it to see if it would suit us. It was a lovely little pub, the publican's wife was nearly in tears when she was talking to us. She said that she didn't want to leave, but her husband had taken over a larger place and was actually there in charge.

Norah and Mollie, 1933

My Little Lady was charmed with it and I thought that we would be very comfortable and happy there and that the girls would be also. We felt quite confident on our way back home in the car, called at Market Harborough for lunch, then on through Lutterworth to Nuneaton. The family were all delighted when we described the place.

But again our hopes were dashed, the next week we had a letter from the brewery informing us that they had appointed a man and his wife who were well-known locally, thanked us for our trouble, and wished us good luck for the future. Such is life, it doesn't do to bank on anything as a certainty, it only disappoints and makes you feel let down when it fails to materialize. We felt sure that the pub was ours.

Norah in 1933

The setbacks which we had met with, over the past fifteen or sixteen years, had not changed my Little Lady much, we were still in love with each other, always good pals, and ready to share each other's burdens. I am rather afraid to admit that I was a lot different in my attitude and outlook to life. I think I was still good-tempered at home, and even tempered in my life away from there, but I was rather cynical in my outlook and my views regarding religious questions and customs of the different Churches, Chapels, and other sections of the religious community. They did not come up to my conception of what true Christianity should be, and what a true Christian ought to do in his everyday life.

The way in which the upper classes, the wealthy people, the big businessmen and the general body of the Church and Chapel going people, went to the Services on the one-day a week, repeating the same prayers, and listening to the same old repetition week after week, not really meaning a word that they were saying, and forgetting all about it during the week (a very large percentage of them, anyway) did not appeal to me. One thing in life that I cannot stand is hypocrisy, and the way in which the better off section of the community ignore and neglect the welfare of living conditions of the lower classes is not my idea of true Christianity. My contention is that everyone is entitled to a fair share of the Earth's bounty. A true Christian should always be ready to give help in some way when it is really needed. This does not always mean in a financial manner, but a helping hand, a smile, encouraging words, a pat on the back, in the knowledge that someone understands, and is ready to help, does a lot of good sometimes. One of the real Christians, and one of the best that I ever met, was a factory worker in Coventry. He was a shop steward, and a red hot communist into the bargain.

Nothing was too much trouble for him, he was always ready to help anyone in trouble or difficulty, and although he had to work hard for his weekly wage, he was on the run all day, straightening somebody's troubles and problems out, although he was handicapped by a very bad rupture. Anyone in serious trouble, financial or otherwise, had only got to mention it to good old G., and he would organise something to help them.

Chapter 32

The Germans were beginning to boast about the might of their nation, and its Army and Navy and Air Force. In addition their industries were flourishing, the exports of their goods were swamping the markets all over the world, undercutting the price of our goods, with the result that it seriously reduced our export trade, which, added up to the unemployment problem, caused business men more trouble.

Every night the German's National Radio programmes were being broadcasted on worldwide wavelengths from nearly midnight until the early hours of the morning, really good class programs of music, all kinds, interspaced with propaganda about their industries, youth movements, social services, and the aims and efforts of the German nation. Neither Britain, or the United States, made any attempt to stop these two dictators or interfere with them in any way, which made them more vainglorious and self assured.

The feeble efforts of Baldwin, Chamberlain and company to stave off Hitler's ambitious ideas of controlling European affairs were of no avail. When Hitler and Mussolini came to terms, and agreed to stand by each other, the Tories began to waken up, and take notice of the dangerous situation that was developing. The aircraft industry was speeded up, civil defence preparations and training began, air raid shelters constructed, hospitals overhauled and re-equipped, new ones built, and large armament factories were built in various parts of the country.

Money was poured into France, to help them construct their Maginot line of underground defence works, which the French Military experts, and ours, thought would be capable of stopping any attempt of invasion by the

German army. How futile these costly preparations were. The Germans invaded Belgium and came round behind the so-called impregnable line when the Second World War started in 1939.

For the first few months of 1939, plenty of people scoffed at anyone who thought that another war was developing, and only needed a spark to set all Europe on fire. But Hitler meant to try and dominate central Europe, and he had done everything possible to build up the German Air Force, Army, and Navy. They were much better equipped than ours, and in addition, the officers and men were all roused by his speeches and enthusiasm to fever pitch.

When the news came to the British nation that we were at war again, the people could not realise that it was true for a time, they were stunned. But when France was over-run, and our small army withdrawn with terrible losses, everyone knew that we were up against it, and almost alone. Our Government was still plodding along in their old tinpot way, and did not waken up, until Hitler began to show his intentions.

Owing to the difficulty of obtaining really good feature films, my brother and his wife were considering selling the Palace Cinema, but they had a very good offer from the Emery Circuit, to take it over on a long lease, so the deal was completed. They still ran the old cinema as a dance hall, it was very popular and paid well. The new firm did not make any staff changes, and everything went along smoothly. As they had quite a number of cinemas in their Circuit, it gave them a better chance of obtaining some really good films, which small, one-cinema proprietors could not obtain.

In 1938, I received notice from the Borough Town Clerk that the four cottages which were up the yard, adjoining our garden, and belonging to me, were included in the clearance scheme for the district. I could see that there was going to be some more trouble, so I got in touch with an estate agent, in order to get rid of the lot before they were condemned, and the tenants moved out of them. We got in touch with several likely firms, but the world situation was so serious and involved, we could not obtain any definite or favourable offers.

In the latter part of the year, the Inspector from the Ministry of Health came to inspect the cottages, and I went round with him. I pointed out to him the improvements that I was prepared to make, and also that they represented the whole of my lifetime savings. He told me not to worry, he would see that I received fair compensation if they were condemned. The enquiry was held later, in the Council Chamber, along with a lot more cases and I was given to understand that fair compensation would be paid, some time later on. The tenants were moved out shortly after, but the compensation never materialised, and it was years before I made a deal with the Borough Corporation, and sold the house and shop, and the cottages, for the same amount that I paid for them in the first instance.

The cottages stood empty all through the war, and for many years after, when the housing problem was so acute and I could have let them all scores of times, to people who would have been glad to stand the cost of repairing and decorating them, but the red tape was too strong, so it could not be done.

A word of advice to anyone, who gets involved in any deal or agreement with Government or Municipal officials, always get the terms or statements in writing, dated and signed, by the official concerned. Don't place any reliance on word of mouth, they will hedge and back out when it comes to the settling point. Not only myself, but lots of other people have found out that this safeguard is needed.

When it was definitely announced that we were at war, on September 3, 1939, the Manager of the cinema, Mr. W., paid all the staff their weekly wage, told everyone that all contracts were broken, that the cinema was closing down temporarily, gave everyone their Unemployment and Health Insurance Cards, and said that we were to sign on at the Labour Exchange. They all took it without any complaint, except me, and I told him that we were entitled to a week's wages in view of notice, and also that I was entitled to another week's wages, holiday pay, as I had not had my annual holiday. He said that he couldn't do anything about it, the Head Office had sent the instructions to him.

I went to the Labour Exchange, and signed on, but I was not satisfied with the way in which the Emery Circuit had treated us, so I wrote to the Head Office, and made a claim for two weeks wages. They ignored my letter, and as we had not the union in the district to back me up, that was that. When the cinema reopened a week or two afterwards, the Manager called and informed me that the Head Office had sent orders to him, that I was not to re-start again. He thanked me for all the help I had given him, wished me luck, and told me that I could always refer to him and said that my wife and I could always go in free whenever we wanted to.

The same week my Little Lady bought one of the Coventry evening papers in which there was an advert for a Steward and Stewardess for the ------ Workingmen's Club.[35] I made an application, and we were asked to go for an interview at the end of the week. The place seemed alright, the terms offered seemed good at the time, so we accepted the position in spite of the fact that the Committee wanted us to take over at once.

---

[35] *George didn't include the name, to protect people alive at the time. It was the Vauxhall Club, in Foleshill.*

I put an advert in our local paper to try and sell the business, but owing to the War we could not find a client, so we cleared all the stock, let the shop to another shopkeeper who was being forced to close down in another part of the town by reason of a clearance scheme.

I went to the Club, and took charge on my own for about two weeks, while my wife and the girls cleared some of the stock at cut prices and packed the remainder to bring with them. What a time I had, getting used to the run of the place, doing the cellar work, cleaning the bar up, stocking it up, serving in the bar with the addition of some help, and keeping my eye on the cash and on the stock, it's very apt to 'leak'. I about wore myself out. In addition to all the work, there was the blackout regulation to comply with, and I was wandering about the store-places, and the Club, until the early hours of the morning to make sure that everywhere was locked up securely, and in no danger from fire. When I did get to bed, I was almost afraid to go to sleep for fear that I should sleep too long, after all, I was fifty-four years of age.

Chapter 33

This short time soon passed, the van came with our furniture, etc., and my Little Lady followed. Was I glad to see her, I'll say I was, it seemed like Paradise to look at her smiling face again. We would be together again, starting on another episode, which increased our knowledge and business experience more than we thought possible.

Norah and Mollie were still going to carry on with their work, travelling to and from Nuneaton, but they both helped in the house and the Club at night-time when needed, and also gave us a lot of help at weekends, which were busy times.

Gertie with Audrey, late 1930s

Audrey was still going to school, but she helped her mother in the daytime and was usually with her when she was busy in the Club. The house where we lived adjoined the Club, it was fairly comfortable, and my wife and the girls soon made it look nice and cosy. The only snag was that the work, which had to be done to keep everywhere and everything up to the mark, left very little time to relax and enjoy it.

The Club was a rather large, ordinary looking building, situated on the corner of a main road, and another short road which led off it. The number of registered members at that time was over 8,000, and it was always very busy, especially from Friday night until Tuesday, when trade quietened down a bit. It was a big, rambling place, store sheds scattered all over the place, some quite a distance from the Club premises, wooden sheds, very insecurely locked, which very easily could have been broken into. There were no proper cellars, one had been made in the yard, sunk into the ground about four feet, and the other was one which had been made out of one of the rooms on the ground floor. The spirit store room joined this one, and the locks were very cheapjack things, not good enough to safeguard the cellars, nor the stock.

I took the Secretary round the place the first week I was there, and told him that I was not going to be responsible for loss of stock unless these places were made more secure. He agreed to have the door strengthened, and told me to get some better padlocks as well.

When we had all got used to the run of the place, and got to know the members, their likes and dislikes, how to handle the stock, and keep the ales etc., in good condition, life became normal again, and we began to enjoy ourselves once more. Club life is entirely different from that in a public house. The atmosphere is more friendly, the restrictions are not so strict, and the members can enjoy card games, dominoes, snooker, billiards, or darts, without any danger of police interference, or the Gaming Laws.

The Steward is always classed as the servant of the members, he cannot assert his authority like a public house licensee. The Committee Members are supposed to help keep good order, while the doorman keeps a check on the visitors and members, so that there is no breach of the law.

There was a lovely big bar on the ground floor, well fitted up, two sets of four beer pumps, good washing-up arrangements, hot and cold water, and plenty of shelves for the glasses in stock. This bar could be entirely closed up and locked, so that the members who wanted to stop on after time could do so, and the Steward could get on with some of the work, and know that the stock would be safe while he was away. There was also another bar upstairs, which was not so well fitted. This was used at weekends, to supply drinks in a very big concert room, which held several hundred people. Four waiters looked after these, and kept my Little Lady and her assistants very busy all the time. Artists were engaged to sing and entertain, etc.

The bar on the ground floor kept me and the barman busy all the time, and in addition, I had to keep my eye on the cash and stock, and on the cellars as well. Sunday dinner time opening was always very busy, there were always about 200 members in the Club, ready for the bar to open up. My barman was a big strong chap, very active and well liked by the members. His one big fault was that he could not stand up to lots of ale, and he had got his pint glass on the go all the time.

My wife's brother, Sid, came over from Nuneaton every weekend to help us, and as he was used to bar work he was able to assist my wife in the top bar, and help to keep an eye on the waiters. The waiters were all good

211

chaps, very helpful, but knowing human nature like I did, I thought it the best policy not to have any loophole for leakage.

I went to Nuneaton on one of my days off and called at the cinema to see my pals. While I was there, the Manager came and had a word with me. He said that he was sorry that I was not on the staff with him, things didn't seem the same. I told them that I was doing well and if the Area Supervisor had been present, I would have treated him to a good cigar for stopping me, it had been a blessing in disguise, and got me out of a rut.

Now for a description of some of the members, and some of the episodes which happened during our short stay.

The President of the Club was a big, self assured sort of man, easy to get on with if he had his own way, but he did not like anyone who knew a bit more than he did. Club life was his hobby and sole interest apart from his business.

The Secretary-Treasurer was another devoted Club man. He made a very big job of the work involved, very slow and painstaking, I could have done all that was needed in half the time. The Committee were all working men, all sorts and conditions, and all enthusiastic Club men.

The Club was controlled by the President, the Secretary, who was also the Treasurer, and the committee, numbering about twelve. All the affairs of the Club were conducted in secrecy, the accounts received and paid by the Treasurer, who worked hand in glove with the President, and kept everything under lock and key.

The price of the goods, discounts, allowances etc., were not shown to the Steward, yet he was expected to show a good margin of profit. This was one side of the business that I did not like. To make any business pay, there must be a large enough selling price over the cost price, which will produce enough surplus to meet all the standing charges and allow for breakages and leakage. The bar prices were fixed by the Secretary and the Committee and were too low, in my opinion, to carry the large amount of all these charges, in addition to repairs, replacements, and other incidentals.

After I had been there for three or four weeks, the President asked me to have a word or two with him in the office, so I went up to see him. He said that the Committee were very pleased with the way in which we were conducting the Club, but they wanted to know when I was going to hand over the £50 Bond money, as security. I told him that until I was sure that there were no loopholes for leakage, then I would consider it. I also told him that the bar prices were too low, no allowance for waste, and that it was impossible to get 36 gallons out of a barrel: there was the bottoms in the barrel, and the leakage when the barrel was bored and vent plugs put in to allow the beer to ferment and then settle down.

We agreed to let the matter stand over for a time, but I did not feel satisfied, they expected too much. The work was hard, the hours long, and both my wife and I were on the go from morning until after midnight, but we enjoyed the life and the company. We had a charwoman to do the cleaning, and we did all the bar work etc., in the midweek. There wasn't any time to brood or bemoan your fate.

At the end of the bar, there was a nice cosy corner, which was always occupied at night-time by the same people. They looked daggers at any other member who intruded on their domain; they were all good company, and all of them inveterate snuff-takers.

One of them was a jolly old chap who told me that he was one of the best upholsterers in the district. He was also one of the oldest members. I had several good talks to him, he made me laugh every time he went home, for he would come up to the counter and say quietly, "Remember what I have told you, you won't last long, they'll kick your arse out of here, you know too much for these buggers." Several ex-stewards called in at different times and they all told me the same tale, that it was impossible to make the margin of profit which the President and his co-partners expected, and advised me not to think of the position as a secure and safe job.

The blackout regulations were very strictly enforced in Coventry, and we were very close to a very large armament works. There were about ten large windows, and the Secretary wanted me to take all the material down from the windows every day, and put them up again at evening time. I told him that I was not going to hold myself responsible for this, and that the Committee could do it.

One of the members was a highly paid engineer. He came in every night, was always in all the weekend, and always stood up against the counter. He was a very heavy drinker, and his language was vile when he began to get over the mark. The first Saturday night that I was in the bar, my wife had not joined me at that time, but there were some other members' wives in the bar room. Towards 10 o'clock, this man started to let go with his vile language, and I asked the barman if he did this regularly. I had heard him in the week time, but as there were no ladies present, it didn't matter so much. The barman said that he was always the same, especially when he had one over the eight.

When this man, his name was D., came in the next Monday night I had a quiet word or two with him and told him to cut his vile language out, especially when ladies were present. He said, "What the hell is it to do with you, you are only the Steward, you are not my boss." I replied, "Well, D----, I told you there is no need at all to

214

use filthy language, I don't object to ordinary swear words, but my wife and daughters will be in the bar next week, they are not used to that sort of talk, and if you don't cut it out, I shall not serve you with any drink, so you can think it over." He blustered a bit, said that he would see the Committee, and see if I was the boss.

When my Little Lady joined me, and came into the bar, he was leaning on the counter as usual. I called her to me and said, "This is my wife, D., I hope you won't shock or disgust her." He looked at me and smiled, "It's all right, George, you needn't worry yourself, I'll behave myself."

He was always very nice to my wife and daughters, though he did let go at times when they were not there. This episode, and several other little efforts to keep the atmosphere cool, boosted my stock with a good many of the members, who enjoyed a few drinks without a lot of filthy language.

Another of the members was a little hunch backed man, he had no politeness, civility, or courtesy. One day was when I was in the bar fairly busy, and not in a very good frame of mind, he came up to the counter, and shouted "Fill me a pint." I said "Alright, wait a minute, it's not your turn." Again he shouted "Come on, Dad, fill my pint." I filled his pint, took his money, and told him, "When you speak to me, my name is Mr. Clarke, or otherwise George, or Steward, I'm not your Dad, and in any case, if I had had a son like you, I would have strangled him at birth."

One Saturday night, I went up to the top bar, to see if my Little Lady was all right, and one of the waiters was bawling out and telling them to liven up. I asked what was wrong, and this waiter said that the customers were waiting for their drinks. I told him, "Let them wait, they can't all be served at once, also, don't you hang about

215

until you want about twenty or more drinks at once. And another thing, don't bawl at my wife, or you won't last long, we can do without such as you."

Shortly after he came down to the bottom bar and told me that he did not like my attitude. The Committee appointed the waiters, paid them, and that I was not his boss. I replied, "Go report me to the Committee if you like, but remember this, I'm in charge here, and you will do what I want you to do, if you don't, you can pack up, now bugger off." This cleared the air with a waiters, it did them all good, they were very courteous and helpful to my wife (and me) after this upset.

These waiters carried their drinks on a large tray with handles on each end. Sometimes, if they hung about, their order would be about sixteen pints of ale, eight or ten Guinness, and about ten glasses of spirits or wine. Each waiter was given £5-0-0 worth of mixed change, they paid for the tray of drinks before they left the bar and collected the money from the customer, so the persons behind the bar had to be quick, sharp and very accurate in their reckoning up, or the waiters would 'twist' them. I told all of them to be honest and straight-forward, and we would get on well together, but if I found any of them on the 'twist', they would hear their name with knobs on, and finish at once.

The cleanliness of the club had been badly neglected and it took several weeks of real hard work before we got it to our own liking, even then, it did not come up to my idea of what a club should be, but it was certainly better.

Chapter 34

The main selling ale was that which came from a brewery at Hook Norton, close to Banbury. It was really good ale, plenty of body in it, strong and potent, and easy to get into good condition. The members called it 'Hooky'. The other ale was a very dark mild, from a Leicester brewery, stronger and good, but very difficult to get into good condition, it wasn't very lively. Guinness Stout was in very big demand and bottled ale, minerals, spirits and wines as well. Keeping a check on the money was fairly easy, but the stock was a different matter. It was scattered about in so many different places, and the blackout gave plenty of opportunity to anyone who knew the run of the place (and there were scores who did know), to be light fingered.

At the back of the club premises, there was a lovely big bowling green, sunken by about a yard, surrounded by a grass bank all round, with stone steps in several places up to the tarmac footpath which ran nearly all the way round it. Large flower garden vases were spaced here and there alongside the path and poplar trees were growing on two sides of the green. I always went up there in the early part of the morning and last thing at night, the breeze was lovely after being in the stale atmosphere so long, and when it was blowing really hard, it whistled through the poplar trees and I thoroughly enjoyed the change.

There was a qualified stock taker who came every three or four weeks and on the results of his check-up, the President and the Secretary-Treasurer knew what profit had been made, and reported to the Committee at their regular meetings. I did not like the idea of the Secretary holding the office of Treasurer as well, there was too much scope for a bit of fiddling, especially when the President was a co-partner. It was quite an easy matter to enter some items, draw discounts, double artist's fees, etc., and the bar takings would have to stand the racket, but the profits would be down and the Steward would be blamed and he could not dispute the statements of the stocktaker. I knew that the amount of trade we were doing, the way in which I work my cellars, spirits and the wines (I need not describe how) the profit ought to have been satisfactory and also cover a certain amount of leakage. In addition the bar prices were too low. Perhaps readers will think that I am giving too many minor details, but they will prove useful to anyone who is considering taking a position as a club steward. There's plenty of work and worry, but not much glory.

On one of my days off, I went into Coventry to have a look round and cash some vouchers. I had a walk round the Cathedral, and then up one of the main shopping streets, going very slowly and looking at windows that interested me. When I got towards the end of the street, I turned down a side street and shortly after heard someone behind me, who was evidently following. When I turned round, two plain clothes men came up to me and asked if they could have a few words with me.

I said, "Certainly, what do you want to know?" One of them then asked me, "What have you been looking in all the shop windows for, we have followed you from the past half-hour." I replied, "That's none of your business, but I am really looking for Johnson and Masons, I've got some business to do with them, though why I should let you know is beyond my comprehension, what right have you to question me about what I'm doing?" They both said, "We are police officers, so will you tell us what your name is, where you live, and what your business is? Here's our badge, so please answer these questions."

I told them that my name was George Clarke, (which made both of them wink at each other) and that I was Club Steward at -------, just outside Coventry. They asked me why I couldn't find Johnson and Masons, when I lived so near to Coventry, and that I had just walked by that firm's premises on the other side of the street. These queries didn't cause me any alarm, in fact, I was enjoying it to a certain extent, so I said to them, "Before we go any further, I want to know what you have got against me, and also, what do you think I'm going to do?" One of them pulled a photograph out of his pocket, and asked if I would take my hat off. I did so, they both winked at each other again, and looked as if they had 'clicked'. The senior of the two then told me as follows, "We are looking for a man named John Clark, about 5 feet in height, rather bald on top of the head, walks with a limp and uses a walking stick, this is his photograph." I looked at it and it was not like me at all, so I said, "Well, what about it, I'm a bit better looking than this bugger, at least I hope so."

They asked me if I would go back with them to Johnson and Masons, to get someone there to back my statements, so I asked them what this man had been doing. They said he had been going round shopkeepers and obtaining money from some of them under false pretences. I told them to lead the way to the firm and I would follow, I said "I am not going to walk between two big buggers like you."

They laughed and we went back to Johnson and Masons. When we got in the retail department, I asked a girl in charge to call the manager in, but she said that he was away for the day and he was the only one on the staff who knew me. The senior man said to his pal, "Stop here with him, I'll get on the phone, and check up with the club."

While he was away one of the lorrymen who delivered the spirits, Guinness etc., to the club came in. I called him, "Jock, will you tell this 'tec' who I am, and what I do for a living?" He said, "Of course I will, you're Mr. Clarke,

Steward of the club, what's the matter?" I told him, and he told the 'tec' that he had blundered. The senior one came back, and said, "It's all right, I have checked it up with the club, and everything is okay." The other one told him about the lorryman, and they both looked a bit sheepish and crestfallen.

I handed some bottle vouchers to the girl in charge, and received the cash due in exchange. The plain clothes men waited for me outside and said they were sorry if they had worried me. I told them not to let it to cause them any loss of sleep, but if they want any more references as to my personal character they could phone the Mayor of Nuneaton, or my brother, the owner of the Palace Cinema and Ballroom, at Nuneaton. I also said to them, "I haven't got time, or we would have gone to your Superintendent's Office and I would have claimed compensation." They both said, "Don't make any trouble, we feel small enough now, if it was not after closing time for the pubs, we would have bought you one of the best drinks in the house, you're worth it." We all had a real good laugh and I told them to call in and see me when they're in my district, but I never saw them again. This shows how easily a man can be suspected and get into a lot of trouble, if no one can identify him.

The war was now well on its way and the blackout precautions were very strict. The stationary balloons were floating in the air all round Coventry and the districts. New factories were being built, old ones altered and reconstructed, to carry on with the manufacture of aircraft and armaments. The enormous engineering works close to the club were working shifts all round the clock.

The weather was beginning to get very cold and I told the President and the Secretary that the bottled goods in the outside store sheds would need to be kept fairly warm, or there would be some trouble through burst bottles. They didn't do anything about it, so I covered the cases up with some old sacks. We had everywhere stocked up with as much as the firms would supply ready for the Christmas trade. All the club members were getting ready for a good time, plenty to drink, and there was going to be a good cold spread, free for all of them.

About a fortnight before Christmas, I went into the cellar to tilt a barrel (i.e. to lift the back end of the barrel up high enough so that nearly all the contents can be pulled by the beer pumps through the tap in the barrel). It was in a rather awkward place and there was rather more in than I thought, while leaning over the barrel pressing down on the front end with my chest and lifting up the back end with my right hand, there was a slight cracking noise and I knew that I had either broken or cracked my ribs.

I carried on until closing time, then did my cellar work, and put everything right for the next day, as I did not know how things would be the next morning, the pain was very sharp and severe.

I did not tell my Little Lady until we went to bed and then I asked her to put a very broad band around my chest and ribs. So she got a long bolster case, cut it and made a long broad bandage. This was wound tightly round me, fastened with large safety pins, and I felt much more comfortable. I got up the next morning, and carried on as usual though I dare not lift anything very heavy for several days, which made a bit more work for my wife and the charwoman, but they did it cheerfully.

We were very busy all through Christmas, both bars were going all the time, the club Brass Band played carols and all the popular tunes, one of which was 'Roll Out The Barrel.' All the members had a real good time, and the only chance we had to relax was when the club was closed, and everything got ready for the next day. After four or five days hard going, the President said they would want the top bar opening one more night, the members wanted to hold a dance. So I said, "You're doing it a bit thick, aren't you, it's the weekend again in two days." He said, "Never mind, we shall pay you for it."

The dance was going on until the early morning, so I went up to the room, and said to the President, "Mr -, it's time you cleared these people off the premises, I want to lock up, and get my work done ready for tomorrow, we've had a hard week". He replied, "It's all right, Mr. Clarke, we shall not be long, you always have to give way a little at these times, it's the festive season." I told him, "That's all right, but from what I can see of this place, it's all give and no take."

After another busy weekend, and the New Year celebrations, I was in the bar on the Friday morning, when in walked a stocktaker. I said "Good Morning, you're here quite early." He replied, "Yes, I am, I'm very sorry you're leaving, Mr. Clarke." I said, "Leaving, who told you that fairy tale?" He replied, "Didn't you know, that's why I'm so early, I want all your cash, and your float." Just then the Secretary and another man came in, and said, "I'm sorry, Mr. Clarke, this is the new Steward, give him the keys and show him around." I said, "Like hell I will, here are the keys, he can find his way around himself, like I had to do, but there's one thing, he will find it more straightforward and a bloody sight cleaner than it was when I took over." My wife came into the bar, and I told her not to do any more work, we had got the sack. I asked her to stop in the bar while I fetched the money, and the Secretary held out his hand, and said, "I'm very sorry Mr. Clarke." I ignored his hand and replied "I neither want you, or your sympathy, both you and the President are a pair of bloody twisters". I went for the bar takings, took my wages out, and also 'riddled' it well, before handing it over to the stocktaker.

Then my Little Lady and I went back to the house to talk matters over. When we got there, she said, "Have a drink, you can do with one, so can I," and pulled a half bottle of whisky out of her pocket, "I took this off the shelf while their backs were turned." I realised then that what old 'G', and the ex-stewards had been telling me was all true, such people are not worth working for.

I told my Little Lady not to worry, there were plenty of good jobs waiting to be taken and that I would soon get fixed up again. We would go back to Nuneaton to live, and be more away from the danger of air raids and bombs. Norah and Mollie started to look for a vacant house, as we did not want to go back to the house and shop on Coton Road, in any case, it would have taken too long to get the tenants out.

There was a Committee meeting at the club the following week, so I went to see them. They were all seated round the room when I went in, like a group of magistrates. I asked why they had acted in such a sudden and dirty manner, without any warning, especially after all the work we put in to get the place clean, in addition, the amount of time and work done during Christmas, before and afterwards.

The President said that the reason was that I had not handed over the bond money, also, that the margin of profit was too low. I asked him, "Have you any complaint about the way in which we've looked after the club, the condition of the ale, beer, spirits, wines etc., or the way in which we have served the members?" He replied, "No, Mr Clarke, everything has been very satisfactory, but the amount of profit has decreased, so we thought it best to make a change." I said, "Are you accusing me of mis-feasance ?" The reply was, "Oh no, it's simply that we cannot carry on unless the profits come up to a certain percentage, the standing charges are very heavy."

I told them then, what I had told both the President and the Secretary-Treasurer some time back, that prices are too low, but no allowance was made by the breweries for loss through tops and bottoms, that there was too much opportunity for the leakage, and that the stock was too scattered. Then I said that I wanted my week's wages, plus the addition for extra work at Christmas, also, one week's wages in lieu of notice, as I'd paid out all that was due to our helpers. The President said that the Committee had decided not to pay any wages, it was their rule to stop a Steward immediately and deduct any deficiency from the bond, but as I had not handed my bond over, this was their remedy. I told them I would put the matter into my Solicitor's hands, and he would put them in Court if they didn't pay up, said "Good Night, to all of you, and the 'Soldier's Farewell.'"[36]

The weather began to get very cold and frosty nights were very frequent, but as luck was on our side for once, there was a large stock of coal which had been paid for by the club. I applied for a position at the Daimler Shadow Factory[37], and got fixed up as a Time and Record Clerk.

---

[36] *Soldier's Farewell: A popular poem from World War 1 :*
I've saddled up, and dropped me hooch, I'm going to take the gap,
my Tour of Duty's over mates, and I won't be coming back.
I'm done with diggin' shell scrapes and laying out barbed wire,
I'm sick of setting Claymore Mines, and coming under fire.
So no more Fire Support Base, and no more foot patrols,
and no more eating ration packs, and sleepin' in muddy holes.
I've fired my last machine gun, and ambushed my last track,
I'm sick of all the Army brass, and I sure ain't coming back.
I'll hand my bayonet to the clerk, he ain't seen one before,
and clean my rifle one more time, and return it to the store.
So no more spit and polish, and make sure I get paid,
and sign me from the Regiment, today's my last parade.

[37] *Daimler on Capmartin Road in Coventry were one of the earliest, and most prestigious names in car manufacturing. During the War a satellite manufacturing facility was built (the 'Shadow') with its own railway platform called "The Daimler Halt". The factory worked round the clock, seven days a week making parts for armoured cars and Lancaster bombers.*

The wage was not very large, but there was plenty of overtime, so that make things a bit better, at any rate, I was not out of work.

The first morning that I went to work there, it had snowed very heavily all through the night and the snow was two or three feet deep. I thought to myself, what a life, there was about three quarters of a mile to trudge, but I got through and started on the new job.

We occupied the clubhouse for four weeks rent-free, as well as the free coal, so we had a bit of our own back and also saw some of the new Steward's troubles. At the end of the first fortnight, after severe frosts, the warning that I had given the President and Secretary re the bottled goods in the outside store sheds was correct, they nearly all froze up, and when the thaw came, an enormous number were either burst or cracked, so that would lower the margin of profit a bit more.

We obtained the tenancy of a new house in College Street, Nuneaton, and moved from Coventry with no regrets, but with a bit more knowledge of human nature, also more business experience. The street was quite close to the Railway Station, and the bus route, so that it was very handy for all of us to travel to and from work. So now, off we will go again on another episode.

Chapter 35

My work in the factory was not very difficult, though it took some time to get into the proper routine, and it kept me very busy, but after two or three weeks I got into the swing of it, and being naturally methodical and careful, everything was O.K. After being there a month, I received a rise of five shillings per week. Some few weeks later, I was told by one of the other time clerks that my wage was still five shillings below the top rate, so I applied for this increase and it was given to me. As we were working from 7:30 a.m. till 6 p.m., and also on Sundays, it made quite a lot of overtime, which increased the normal wage and so made things a bit better for the household expenses.

The foreman in charge of the section for which I was doing the time recording was a man named P----. He was a very intelligent, conscientious, level-headed sort of man, rather overbearing and inclined to think that he was always right, but as he was a really clever engineer, this was only natural, there were so many 'duds' about. The factory was a new one, built specially for the production of the Aero engines, and everything was under the supervision of the Air Inspection Department of the Armaments Manufacture Ministry and its Inspectors. Everything needed for the engines, from the tiny screws and washers, up to the larger parts, were made in the factory, and then fitted together in the fitting shop. The engine was then tested and later on fitted into the engine bodywork, ready for the Spitfires.

As the Germans had been over several times and dropped some bombs, rather haphazardly, there were fire drills, and air raid drills. Each section were allotted shelters and marched into these, so that in the event of the factory being bombed, everyone would know what to do.

The factory was about half a mile from the Railway station, and we had to walk across a very large, open common, on which the Germans had dropped a number of bombs. These shell holes were rather large, full of water, and quite open.

One very dark night after working overtime, I started to cross the common, and somehow, got off the footpath. I felt for my pocket torch, but it wasn't in my pocket, I had forgotten it. I wandered round a bit, very slowly, because of the shell holes, but could not find the path again. All at once, I saw just a faint twinkle of light from the railway signals and I thought, now if I could only get to the iron fencing, which ran all the way round the side of the common, alongside the railway track, I can get safely to the footroad which leads to the station. I went very carefully and slowly, and what a relief it was when I reached the iron fence. I was always very careful afterwards, and make sure that my torch was in good order and in my pocket.

During the very severe winter, the snow was about a yard deep on this open common, and in some places where it had drifted, it was six feet or more in depth. When the men were following one another along the footpath in single file, they looked like Indians on the trail, from a distance.

This winter of 1939-1940 was a very severe one, and with coal being very strictly rationed, it made things worse. Everybody, except some of the favoured few, was scratching around for wood, coal slack, or anything that would burn and make a fire. With the road conditions being so bad, more people were using the railways, while hundreds of men and women who had been out of work, or had changed their occupation, were travelling via Nuneaton to Coventry, to help with the War effort. The compartments were packed, most of them with two dozen people in them, instead of the normal dozen. In addition, the guards van was usually packed full of men, all standing up, wedged like sardines. If anyone had got his hands in his pockets, he had got to keep them there, he couldn't get them out until the pressure eased. It was the same if he happened to have lifted his arm or arms up, it was impossible to get them down until some of the men got out. Not one of them fell down, there just wasn't room. It wasn't so bad going to work, as all factories did not start work at the same time, but it was bad enough; it was coming back home when the worst overcrowding occurred, they were all eager to get home and pushed and shoved their way into the compartments, until they could hardly breathe.

On Foleshill station, the platforms were very long and wide, and I have seen them standing 10 or 12 deep the full length of the platform, especially when the trains were late, or on Fridays, pay day. I was in a carriage one day, it was full when we reached Foleshill, but the men started to push in, and one of them got wedged in a doorway. Those behind kept pushing and shouting, "Go on, get in, we don't want to stop here all night." He shouted, "Alright, but I can't go without my bloody arm." He'd got it stretched out along the outside of the compartment, and couldn't shift it.

We were in a very crowded compartment, and one of the men who was standing up kept fumbling about, and said, "That's bloody funny, I could have sworn that I'd got a packet of fags in my pocket, but I can't find them." The man next to him looked at him, and said "You ain't bloody likely to, either, you've been feeling in mine."

I was in a compartment one night with one of my fellow clerks named Harry, he was a testy, short tempered, unreasonable fellow. We had got into the compartment at the Daimler Halt, two stations before Foleshill. Harry said to those in the seats, "We'll have a comfortable journey home tonight, I've got a carriage key, I'm going to lock the door and draw the blinds down, then no one can get in."

I told them that he was not playing the game, that the men wanted to get home as much as he did. When we reached Foleshill station, there was a big crowd waiting and they kept pulling at our door. Eventually the pulling and shaking cause the top part of the window to slide down, and the men clambered through, until the compartment was packed tight, and the train started again. One of the men, a big chap, kept looking round, especially at old Harry, I think someone had "split". This big chap looked very hard at the old man and said, "There's somebody in here that's got a carriage key. If I was sure who it was, I'd throw the bugger through the window, and make him walk home." I looked at Harry, the perspiration was streaming down his face, and his hands were trembling. Next morning, when I saw him at work, I said, "You'll perhaps have a bit more sense now, and consideration for your fellow working men, they all want to get home, you were very lucky, only your age saved you from getting a 'sock' on your jaw."

Two of the girls who were working as time clerks were in the early morning train travelling to work, and the carriage was in darkness, as there had been an air raid warning. It was also very dark outside. The train pulled up between two stations, and the girls thought that they had reached their destination. One of them opened the door, stepped out, and dropped four or five feet onto the railway track. The other girl just stepped back in time, the train started off again, and the girl left in the compartment was too dumbfounded to pull the communication cord. When she got out at the station and informed the Station Master, he went back to search for her sister and met her walking very slowly towards the station. She was very badly bruised, but no bones were broken, so she was very lucky in that respect.

It was nothing unusual for the trains to be held up for one or two hours at night time, when the air raids were on, or warnings that the Germans were coming over. The raiders made a very big effort one night to put all the track out of action. They mis-judged their aim, as for four or five miles on each side of the track, about 30 yards away, the bombs had been dropped in continuous lines, in fields most of them.

Chapter 36

As the months rolled on, the factory managers in Coventry came to an agreement with the bus companies, and works buses were run to and from the factories, which was a big improvement, and relieved the overcrowding on the railways.

The Shadow factory was now beginning to get very busy and the number of people employed was increasing every week. There were all sorts, men and women from most English counties, also from Scotland, Wales, and Ireland, most of them had to be trained, doing the easy simple jobs at first, then put on to more skilled work according to their ability. I did my best to encourage them, as I had to check and record their work-cards. Some of the girls, (and some of the men), who were living in hostels, got fed up and homesick after a week or two, but they soon got over it. A smile, and a few words of encouragement worked wonders with most of them, and the thought of a big wage packet did the rest.

The foreman, P., had many a good talk to me. He said that he and his fellow foremen, about fifteen of them altogether, were not satisfied with the wage that they were getting, as some of the semi-skilled workers were getting much more, and they, the foremen who had trained them, were still responsible for them, and the quality of the work done.

They had several interviews with the manager, who was a very quiet, unassuming sort of man, and he was a bit afraid of the foremen, some of whom were rather loud-mouthed, and aggressive. This manager was moved to another factory, the one who took his place was an unknown quantity, but he soon showed his ability and driving force.

The layout of the different sections of the factory was altered, production speeded up, and some of the foremen were on the 'carpet' for slackness. P. led a small deputation to air their views, also to put forward their claim for an increase. Before he went, he said to me that they were going to show the new manager who was boss. This was in the late afternoon, and when I was leaving the factory to go home (it was my early night), I met P. and he looked a bit crestfallen. I asked how they had got on, if they had obtained their increase and whether the new manager had agreed to their demands. He looked at me, and I could see that he was upset. He said, "No, George, both P. (another foreman) and I have got the sack. He said that we were the ringleaders, we are being paid up tonight, so I shall not see you again." He held out his hand and shook mine, and said "Good Night". There were tears in his eyes, and mine were rather moist.

His charge-hand stepped up into his place, his name was A., he was a good, clever engineer, younger than P., and lacked the driving force and disciplinary power which P. possessed. When he was in the office with me, we talk matters over, and as I had quite a lot of experience in handling men and women, I helped him out as much as I could, to keep things running smoothly.

There was another man on the section who had always been well in with P. He was also a charge-hand, a good engineer, clever and conscientious, his name was H., and he thought that he ought to have been promoted instead of A. He was a really good singer, very much in demand at suppers and dinners, and also at the concerts held in the canteen at the works. He was also a very good gardener, and gave me some very good information which came in very useful. Mushroom growing was one of his hobbies, he told me that when he first started, he made a compost bed all along one side of his greenhouse on the floor, put several lots of mushroom spawn in for more than two years, and got no results, despite following all

232

the instructions. In disgust, he loaded all the bed up onto his barrow, tipped it in a heap at the back of the greenhouse, and forgot all about it. Winter came and passed, and in the spring he was looking round the garden and came to this heap. It was smothered with mushrooms and he said that he gathered lots more during the year. He settled down under A., made the best of his disappointment, and they became good friends.

There was another good chap, who became one of my best pals at the factory. He lived outside Coventry, so that I never had much chance to meet him outside, in any case, there wasn't much time, we were always at work. His name was J., he was of medium height, strong, and very active. He was a good singer and mimic, full of fun, good at football, cricket, darts, and all kinds of sport. He was also a big favourite of the ladies. The third or fourth week I was there, J. came into the office, and asked me whether I wanted to have a go on his fixed odds football ticket, so I had a pound on a five to one shot. He brought me the six pounds in on the next Monday, and said "I'll bring you the ticket in again this week, it looks as if you can sort them out." I asked him at the end of the week for the ticket, and he told me that the bookie would not give him one, and said, "Bugger you, J., we don't want your sort of bets, we should soon be out of business." J. had doubled my bet.

Production was now increasing rapidly under the new Manager, together with the instructions from the Ministry, which allowed the workers to speed up the time taken on the machine jobs, and so increased their bonus allowances. This bonus system enabled the workers to earn very big wages, but the clerical staff, whose work was also largely increased, received no bonus, only their ordinary wage, though we did get an increase, even if it wasn't a lot.

Later on, all the time and record clerks were put on the staff, the wage was increased again, and we were paid our full wages if we had time off through illness, or with the permission of the foreman. This made our position more secure, and cured the unrest.

Of my best friends among the time clerks, was an ex-army captain, named B. He had been badly shot up in the first World War, and has lost one of his legs above the knee. This had been replaced by an artificial one, and B. walked very well with the aid of a good strong walking stick. He was a very well educated man and was rather out of his element among the rank-and-file of the factory workers, though he didn't put on any airs, and was friendly, up to a certain point. The cost of living had compelled him to apply for work, as his pension was not large enough to keep him going, in addition, he had rather expensive tastes, and liked the good things of life.

When he got to know me, he always came and had his lunch in my office, as we enjoyed each other's company. He told me, "I like to talk to you, George, you've been through the mill, like I have, and seen something of what makes life worth living, not like some of these buggers, all they can talk about is work." Like me, he was very fond of horse racing, so we had mutual interests and had many a good laugh at our own mistakes, near misses, and misfortunes. He had been educated at public school, one of his fellow school pals was J.Js., the trainer, but he said, "He is now very aloof, I wish he would thaw out a bit, I might be able then to know when he is '*on the job*'."

When he finished with army life, he joined up with two of his army pals, and they made quite a lot of money buying army surplus goods in bulk, then selling them to small traders and factors at a very good profit. After this he bought an interest in a S. P.[38] bookmakers business, in

[38] *S.P.: Starting or fixed price bookmaking as opposed to the totaliser (Tote) method*

234

the West End of London, but owing to his inexperience, he was robbed, and twisted right and left, lost nearly all his money, and had to pack it up. After I left the factory, I never met him again, and I hope that he pulled through alright. I liked his company, and he seemed so lonely.

Quite a different type of man, was another ex-Army Lieutenant, who also came to be trained as a time clerk (I usually had the trainees to instruct in my office, perhaps because I was more patient, as well as being more methodical, than most of the others). He had been educated at public school, but he could not have been a very brilliant scholar. He was very dull, slow-witted, his writing was very poor, and his knowledge of arithmetic very vague. Considering that he had been in the Army and also an officer, he knew very little about the facts and the ordinary ways of life, and considered the ordinary working man, or woman, as something quite apart from his conception of what people should be like.

When the foreman sent him to me to be trained, he had been in one of the other time offices for four or five weeks, and had not made any progress. The foreman told me that he had seemed hopeless but perhaps I could liven him up and make him good enough for one of the smaller sections. He came, I watched him, and he hadn't learned anything. I asked if he really wanted to become a time clerk. He said that he did, so I told him that he would have to liven up, and take more interest in what was being done and not be afraid to make a mistake, I would correct it. He got my 'back up' lots of times, he was so dense and slow on the uptake, and yet he was so smug in his opinions, and the superiority of the upper classes. Eventually, after several weeks of patient explanations, firm handling, and some occasional 'cussing' bouts, he began to shape a bit better, and the penny began to drop.

I never really liked the man, one reason was that he was so childish, and also, he was a bigoted Tory. We were talking about world affairs one day, the section foreman was with us, and I said that the real wealth of any country depended upon the workers and what they produced, and not entirely on the one pound note. This ex-army man looked at me, and said, "What do you know about finance, or business, if it comes to that?" I replied, "A bloody lot more than you do, or your class, if you are one of the samples." My reply rather nettled him, especially when A., the foreman joined in, and put one or two Socialistic points to him, to which he had no answer.

Later on he said, "Never mind, wait until the War is over, the Conservative Government will know how to deal with men like you two and the rest of the Labour people, who are so cock sure at the present time, they will keep them in place." I told him, "If you think that the Tories will rule the roost again after this lot, you are in for a shock. The Labour Party will sweep the country and the Tories will get the biggest hiding they have ever had, the rank and file of this country of ours are fed up to the teeth with the worship of the upper classes, and the class distinction backed up by the Tory Party."

He was over six feet in height, very well built, but a proper 'sissy', squeaky voice, but no conversationalist, he took no interest in sport, never had a bob on a horse, or football ticket. He liked a drop or two of whisky, but he was a mean bugger, the sort that lets the other man pay twice. Perhaps you will think I have overstepped the mark a bit, and been too critical and fault finding, but as I said before, he was so smug he got my back up, and I never liked him from the start.

Old G.W., the shop steward, and a Communist as well, was a man you couldn't help liking. He was rough and ready, although badly handicapped by a severe rupture, he was always ready to help anyone in trouble and always did his best for newcomers to the factory, looking after their comfort and well-being until they got accustomed to the new job and surroundings.

A., the foreman over the workmen on the section, was another very good sort of man. A clever engineer, very patient and methodical, intelligent in his outlook both about his work and affairs in general. He was very helpful to his workmen, especially to the trainees, some of whom were very slow on the uptake, who need the patience of Job to deal with them and keep them from doing a lot of 'scrap'.

Our job as time and record clerks did not come under the jurisdiction of the Engineering Manager, our Boss was the Chief Accountant and all our orders came from him, via our foreman whom we called Albert. He was a very friendly type of man, very quick and active, he wasn't very tall, carried no weight, and was very highly strung, nervy, in fact, rather jumpy. We got on very well with one another, though we had one or two arguments until he realised that I was able and always willing to do my best. One instance that I remember, we had quite a few heated words over it, but it came to an agreement which cleared the air for both of us.

I had quite a large, busy section to check and record for. One Monday morning, quite a number of workmen from another section came to my office for me to record their time. I asked who had told them to come to my office, and they said that their time clerk told them. I refused to record their work, and told them to go to their own office, I hadn't received any orders. Albert came rushing in to see me, and asked me why I had sent the men back. I told him that in the first place, I had not been told about the additional number, and also, that the amount of work I was doing was quite enough to do thoroughly, for the wage we were getting. If he was going to increase the number of men to me to look after, I would either want an increase in my wages, or additional help in the office.

237

Albert said, "You could cope with the extra work all right, I could do it easily and I know you could." I replied, "You're the one to do it then, I'm not going to make myself a nervous wreck like you did, I came here to work, not kill my bloody self." He went out, very hot under the collar, but the additional men went to another time office, not mine. We understood each other after this and became good friends. I always knew from past experience that the old saying is true, 'Work the willing horse, he'll work till he drops, the rogue can stop in the stable.'

One day, Albert brought a little Welshman into the office and said, "This is Ted, I want you to train him, get him ready as quickly as possible. I want him to go on the night shift, they are a man short." Ted was very willing, but factory work and our own system of timekeeping was a bit beyond him. I pushed him along as fast as I could, and sometimes he would look at me with mournful eyes like a spaniel dog, and say, "Oh, George, leave me alone for a bit, I'm getting all worked up." I said to him, "Now, Ted, you heard what the foreman said to me, you've got to be trained very quickly, the office you go in on the night shift will be very busy, if you watch me and do what I tell you, you will be able to manage all right. You want the job and the wages badly, according to what you told me."

He told me that he would do his best, and that he was very grateful for the help I was giving him. Albert came in towards the end of the week and wanted to know how he was going on, and whether he would be all right at the end of the week to go on a night shift. I told them that Ted was not ready, and that he needed another week's training. However, Albert ignored my advice, sent Ted on the night shift, and the poor little Welshman got bewildered and worried, his record cards were all mixed up, some of the men's time was entered on the wrong cards, and some not entered at all.

When I heard about it, I told Albert that it was his fault, he ought to have let him have another week with me. In addition, I said, "You needn't bring any more trainees to me, if you won't be ruled by my judgement as to whether they are capable of being on their own, it isn't fair to them, and also it isn't fair to me, it makes it look as if I don't know how to teach a man properly." He couldn't retaliate, he knew that he was in the wrong, but he didn't bring any more to me. Ted was moved to another job, and stayed on nights.

During this time, the German raiders were coming over nearly every night, bombs were dropped all round Coventry and district and of course, in other parts of the country as well. They were making a special target of Coventry because of the aircraft and armament industries, and a large proportion of the people had got the wind-up, and the jitters. When the raiders came over, they usually came over Nuneaton first, and nearly every night as soon as we got to bed, the air raid warning would scream out and that would spoil our nights rest till about 3 or 4 a.m., and then it was nearly time to get ready for work again.

Although those who worked on the night shift were in more danger and spent half their working hours in the shelters, they were able to sleep more soundly in the daytime, and some stopped night work, they liked it better. "What a life," not much bed, no sleep, and on rations.

239

Chapter 37

My Little Lady had plenty to do during this period, the girls were all working, and it kept her very busy doing all the household work, running round after the rations, and trying to get something else in addition, to help those meagre quantities out. Somehow, in one way or another, she managed to get me a good hot meal ready, for which, when I landed in home after being away for about fourteen hours on a diet of paste sandwiches, most days, I was very grateful and <u>ready</u> for. During the time I was working such long hours and on Sundays as well, I was too tired to go out anywhere, so my Little Lady had an hour or two with her sister, Charlotte, to pass the time away, and make a bit of change from housework. They usually went and had a drink at our old pub, the King William IV, but my wife said that it didn't seem the same as when we kept it, there wasn't so much fun and life, and lots of our old customers said the same to her.

In the middle of 1940, Norah's fiancé[39] received his notification that he would be called up, so he volunteered, and joined the Royal Warwickshire Regiment, went through a period of intensive training, and was then stationed for some time on the East Coast, near Yarmouth. Norah said that they wished to get married. Both my wife and I were agreeable, and we told them that we would help them as much as we possibly could, also that they could live with us until they were able to set up on their own. They were married on November 14, 1940. It was a quiet little wedding and solemnised at Chilvers Coton Church, where my Little Lady and I were married. We had a nice little party at the Newdegate Arms Hotel and everybody enjoyed themselves. Norah and Oliver did not go away for a

---

[39] *Oliver Betteridge*

honeymoon but booked a room at the hotel, so that they could be on their own, for a short time, anyhow.

Norah with George on her wedding day

**Norah with Oliver Betteridge,
November 14th, 1940**

After the wedding[40]

What a night it was, the German raiders came over, dropped one or two bombs on Nuneaton, which did not do much damage. But Coventry was blitzed, the damage done was terrible and a large number of people lost their lives. Factories and hundreds of houses and shops were damaged, many of them razed to the ground. The Shadow Factory where I worked was badly damaged. The glass roofing all over the factory was all shattered, the factory floor was all covered with twisted iron window stays, broken glass, electric light fittings, cables, and a lot of damaged brickwork. Luckily, this was caused more by blast than by direct hits, and all the machines were intact. All the men who turned up for work were set on to clean up the mess, and the young men had to help the builder's men repair the roof. So well did they work, that

---

[40] *The tall figure second left between Oliver and his mother is Bert Bucknall, standing in for Oliver's father who had died some time earlier.*

the factory was in full production again in just over a week.

A factory close to ours was absolutely blown to bits, and fires burned everything to ashes. To look at it afterwards, it must have been like the "'hellfire' that the Evangelists and others have said sinners and back sliders would have to endure. I had a very narrow escape from death, or very serious injury, while the repairs to the roof, etc., of the factory were in progress. Our offices were made of very thick glass panels, fixed in iron frame-work, closed in all round, and open at the top. Some of the machines on the section were in operation, and I was busy one morning at my desk. An electrician and his mate were working directly overhead, dust and bits of material kept dropping down, so I moved to the right side of the office.

Whether it was luck, or fate, I don't know, but it was a good job that I had moved, as two or three minutes later down came, from the roof an enormous pair of steel pliers, bang onto the desk, and made a hole in the leather covering nearly an inch deep. My head would have been just over that spot if I had not changed my position. The electrician's mate came down the ladder into the office grinning like a Cheshire cat, and said "Anybody hurt? The pliers slipped off the platform." I replied, "No, but they only missed my head by inches, and if I had stopped in my usual place there might have been an inquest, you ought to have cord or light chains attached to your tools from your belt when you're working overhead."

When the German raiders came over, and the sirens started their horrible wailing, my daughters and my wife used to get straight out of bed, dress and get into the shelter. My wife used to say to me, "Come on, George, they are coming over again." I told her to take things more easily, it was time to get into the shelter when the bombs started to drop. In any case, if our name was on one of them, it would get us wherever we might be. It didn't make any difference, they still got up and were out of bed more than they were in. But I could not have carried on with my work without some rest and a little sleep, the hours are too long, and the work too exacting.

Norah (third from left, front)
at the Midland Red

Mollie had now joined the Police Force, and was attached to the Bedworth Division, working in the office, one week on days, and one week on afternoons. I think she enjoyed the change from shop work, there was more change and variety. Norah and Audrey were both working in the offices of the Midland Red Omnibus Company and were very comfortable.

Oliver had gone through some very intensive training, which had made him very fit, and as hard as iron. Some weeks later, Norah had a letter from him, stating that he was fit and well, and that they were in Iraq, and would be there for some time.

In November, Norah told my Little Lady that she would be a Grandmother in 1943. Winter passed, and in the spring of 1943, on March 22nd, Norah gave birth to a bonny boy,[41] and we were all very pleased when this event was over, there had been so much turmoil during the previous year or two, it was a real relief for anything to go on so smoothly. It was quite an event when Norah came back from the hospital, and she had decided to name her son, Thomas Oliver, thus coupling her husband's name, with that of her brother, Tom, whom we so tragically lost when he was nearly 23; so now, we had another Tommy.

Norah with Tommy Betteridge, July 1943

At the factory, orders came through from the Ministry of Fuel and Power, that the consumption of electricity had got to be drastically reduced. When I got in my office one morning, the highly powered lamps had been removed, the smaller lamps put in their place, and the light was about one candlepower. This had been done in all the

---

[41] *Thomas Oliver Betteridge. Tom attended King Edward VI Grammar School from 1954 to 1959, and retired after a long career with Courtaulds. Tom lived in Harrogate, and died there on 17th Sept. 2010.*

time offices, so I asked the clerks what they were going to do about it. They said it was orders, and we have got to put up with it. I had a word with Albert, our foreman, but he said that he couldn't do anything. So I thought, well, old man, it's up to you again.

I rang the Chief Electrician up, but he said that he was only obeying orders, and couldn't do anything. Then I rang our boss, the Chief Accountant, told him that the light would injure our eyesight, and in any case, we could not see to do our own work properly. I told him who I had contacted, and he said that in that case, he didn't think that he could do anything. Then I told him that I didn't intend to have my eyesight ruined, that if a better light was not put in the office, I would walk out at lunchtime, and I shouldn't come back. The electrician came, put the higher powered bulbs back again, just about an hour later. The other time clerks carried on in the dim light for several days, and then they were all changed.

Such minor economies as the above are always being tried out in every factory or other industry, where the workers will stand for it, while power unlimited is wasted in other directions. It is the same with Income Tax, the small man has to pay every penny, while the big 'uns' get away with thousands.

I had now fixed up a seat in one of the buses hired by the management, this picked me up close to home, and went right into the factory yard. It was waiting for us when the shift was over, and this made transport easier, and more comfortable than travelling on the over-crowded trains, though we didn't have so much fun.

One morning in November, when the fog was very thick, our bus was going through one of the new building estates at a snail's pace, and after trailing about for nearly an hour we hadn't reached the factory, so the driver and conductor got out, had a careful look round, and discovered that the driver had been going round and round one of the green circles in the middle of the estate.

The fog, and the weather in general, in 1942, was very bad in the winter, and what with the fuel shortage, food rations, air raids, and warnings, life was not very comfortable, nor easy.

I had a young married woman come to work with me. She was very quick, but awfully jumpy and nervous, I think the air raids had upset her, and she was not very happy in her home life. After a few days she calmed down and was a lot quieter, and told me that working with me had done her more good than all the Doctor's medicine and the nerve tonics that she had been taking, I was so calm and good-tempered. She said that in the other offices, the time clerks were fidgety, jumpy, and irritable, and had made her feel as if she could squeal. Eventually, however, she had to give the job up, as she would never have been able to cope with the work on her own. She was very grateful for my help.

Another young woman who came to work with me was named Sylvia. She was very brisk and confident, and we got on very well together. She did a good share of the work, and would have done it all without any trouble if I had let her. Before coming into the factory, she had been a Probationary Nurse in one of the hospitals. We had many a good laugh together over some of our experiences, and what we had seen in the hospitals. Sylvia said that when she was helping in the operating room at the hospital, the first few weeks were terrible, and that she nearly collapsed several times, her legs were like jelly. One day the surgeon was amputating a man's leg, and Sylvia was holding and steadying the leg. When the surgeon had completed the operation she said, "There was I, standing with a leg in my hands, my knees knocking together, and I was ready to fall on the floor. I said to the surgeon, "Wha-, wha-, what have I got to do with this?" He looked at her, smiled, and said, "There is no need to be frightened, it won't bite you, put it in that bucket of antiseptic over there." When she left the hospital, she went as a nurse at a private nursing home for the elderly, and awkward, rich old women.

One night when she was on duty by herself, she said that she felt frightened to death, and hardly dare go on her inspection round along the long, dimly lit corridor. The patients all had separate rooms of their own, and some of them, who were addicted to wandering about, were always locked in. Sylvia reached the end room of the corridor, unlocked the door, reached inside the room to switch the light on, and her hand came in contact with somebody's cold face. When she switched the light on, there was the old lady standing there fully dressed, she said that she was going home. Sylvia told me, "George, it nearly killed me, I was ready to faint, but I pulled myself together and persuaded her to get into bed again." We always enjoyed each other's company, and were always good pals, for two or three years. She would make someone a good wife, she was so full of courage, life, fun and jollity.

Some of the girls and young married women who were working in our factory, and the other factories as well, had their heads turned by some of the married men who are working with them, carried on illicit love or lustful affairs, which often ended, more often than not, in disillusionment and sometimes, nine months of misery and an unwanted child at the end of that period.

Two sisters who worked in our factory were both very nice girls, and were helping to support their widowed mother, who idolised both of them. The eldest of the two, Mary, was a very level headed girl, and she came in to see me and asked me to have a good talk to her sister, who was having an affair with one of the foremen, a young married man, who was very fond of the ladies. She came into my office every day to collect the work cards (I'm talking about the younger one), and I said, "Sit down, Kathleen, I want to talk to you." She replied, "It's no use, George, I know what you want to talk to me about, it won't do any good." I said to her, "Now, my dear, listen to me, I've got three daughters of my own, and I don't want you to end up in trouble, which is generally the result of these affairs, it would break your mother's heart, and also ruin your own life. This man you are infatuated with is no good, and when he has obtained what he's after, he will drop you in the mud, and leave you to bear the shame and burden alone."

Kathleen looked at me, started to cry, and then I said, "Pack it up, my dear, while you are all right, he isn't worth bothering about, there are plenty of nice young single men, who would be pleased to take you out, and make a match of it, if you wish." She went out of the office, and her sister told me a day or two later that the affair was now ended. Don Juan went by the office several times, gave me some black looks, but didn't say anything. I was ready for him if he had done so, and he would have heard a few particulars about his personal character, which he would not have relished.

Production kept on the increase from our factory, and this was the result of the Works Manager's drive, assisted by some young energetic members of staff, one of whom was a real live wire. This was a tall, well built young man named Bill, and he was very friendly with me. He was the Assistant Works Manager, full of energy, ideas, fun; games appealed to him when we had time for them, and the ladies came in for special attention, he always found time for them.

One day, in the office, I had sorted some horses out of the morning paper, and I was writing my commission out, and I heard someone behind me, it was Bill, he was looking over my shoulder. He said, "You might as well tear that up, save your money, because those buggers won't win." I replied, "Not likely, I shall have a bundle to come back, take a copy of these, and back 'em yourself." He said, "No thanks, but put Hycilla with yours, if you want a good priced winner." I didn't include Hycilla, and it won at ten to one. My ticket clicked, and I won nearly £100. If I had included Hycilla, the bookie would have died from shock.

Bill came by the next morning, looked in the office, and said, "You lucky old bugger, and what did you hit him for, I wish I had taken your advice, and copied your bet."

Some of the men in the factory were very heavy gamblers. They were earning good wages, and after handing over their housekeeping shares to their wives, had always plenty left for drink and gambling, all sorts, horseracing, dog racing, card playing, football tickets and pools. They would put a fiver on a horse or a dog as casually as it was only five bob. One of the men, whom I talked to quite a lot, was a very heavy gambler. He had a really good run of luck, and then it changed, he lost, day after day, and instead of slowing down, he chased his losses and lost all his money.

There was a young woman in charge of the department which typed all the details of the works cards used by the operators of the machines to record the time taken on jobs. She was a very good-looking woman, half French, her mother was a French woman. Every day, she walked up the centre gangway of the factory from her office to the main set of offices at the other end. She wore a black dress of very soft clinging material, which accentuated all the curves in the right places, she had large showy earrings, bracelets on her wrists, and her ankles. As she walked through the factory, all the men were watching her, and the whistling and wolf calls were one continual chorus. They called her the production stopper. After about a couple of weeks, the Works Manager informed her that she had got to walk up the drive outside the factory, as she caused too much distraction and comment.

Chapter 38

During that time I had been at Coventry, one thing I noticed about the majority of the men who worked there was that their main ambition was to get as much money as possible. The old time pride in craftsmanship had gone, and all that mattered, was the bottom line on their weekly pay ticket.

The only safeguard against shoddy and bad work was the strict supervision by the Inspection department, or more than half of the work would have been inferior or scrap. The bonus system brought about more production, but some of these semi-skilled operators, or engineers as they classed themselves, were responsible for a large amount of breakage of valuable machine tools, in their eagerness to obtain as much bonus as possible. I don't know whether I have got a grudge against them, or not, but we did not get any bonus, perhaps that was the reason, but I always thought as I looked at them, that most of them developed an acquisitive look on their face, which showed up more than ever on pay days.

They were generous, up to a point, but sometimes they were rather mean, admitted there was always some subscription list nearly every week, and often a collection for some cause or other as well, a couple or three bob was nothing to them, but they wouldn't part with that much, a 'tanner' was more in their line.

To illustrate my point, just one episode. One of the foremen, through ill-health, was leaving the factory to take up an outdoor job. He had been a very good friend to all the operators in his section, looking after them, and putting pounds and pounds in their way. They went round with a subscription list for him, to obtain a present for him when he terminated his employment. The two men who had been collecting came into my office, and I asked them how they had got on. One of them said, "We've done well, more than £10, and there's still a bit more to come in, don't you think so George?" I replied, "So you think that's good, I think it's a disgrace to the section, what does it run to the number on the three shifts, about a bob each? what a reward for the foreman, he has looked after all of you, put you right when blunders have been made, put pounds into all your pockets, you all ought to feel ashamed of yourselves."

The women workers in the factory were much more generous if they were doing well, they always handed a couple of bob over at holiday times, and said "Have a drink with me, George, it will do you good."

One young Scotch girl was very frightened when she first started. I talked to her, and explained as much as I could about the work. This made things easier for her, she soon got topside her job, and settled down nicely. When Christmas came, she went home to Glasgow for the holiday to visit her parents. When she came back, she came into the office and told me that she had mentioned how helpful I had been to her parents, and that her mother had sent me a large spray of white heather, to bring me good luck.

Whether it was lucky for me or not, I do not know, but Nuneaton had a very disastrous air-raid on May 17th, 1941, large numbers of houses and shops were either absolutely blown to bits, or very badly damaged. Chilvers Coton (Shepperton) Church was almost destroyed, only the Belfry and Clock tower remained standing, although badly damaged.

On the night of the Blitz, my Little Lady and I were in bed when the air-raid warning sounded. As usual, she got up at once; while she was dressing she walked to the bedroom window, looked out, and then said, "You'd better get up, George, Nuneaton is one great mass of lights."

Our Street is one of the highest parts round Nuneaton, and when I got out of bed and looked through the window, it was just like fairy-land, flares were dropping everywhere, two or three different colours, landing on the houses, settling on the trees, and hedges. We went downstairs, the girls were already in the shelter, and then we heard the German bombers coming over. We went into the pantry, which is under the staircase, and almost at once, the bomb came 'zooming' down, which caused the damage to Coton Church, and numerous houses in the vicinity. As we were listening to the sound, we both thought the same, this is the finish of all of us.

Chilvers Coton Church after the air raid, 1941

But it dropped two or three hundred yards from our street, there was a roar, then a crash, both our front and back doors were violently blown open by the blast, and a large lump of stone came through the roof, and dropped onto the bedroom floor, about a yard away from our bed. The bed was smothered with plaster and laths, and the stone would have gone right through the bedroom floor into the entrance hall, if it had not lodged on the partition

255

wall. Incidentally, I always got up, afterwards, when the air-raid warnings came through.

Church Street, Nuneaton, 1941

My brother, Sid, who was a warden for his district, was out on duty with a fellow warden in Queens Road. A bomb came down, destroyed a lot of property. Poor old Sid and his pal, were killed instantly by the effects of the blast. Numerous families were absolutely wiped out, and in some cases, where the husband or father was out on night work, he returned to find his home gone, and in some cases, his wife and children dead, or badly injured.

Then the 'big nobs', and most of the clergy, prate about 'Peace on earth, goodwill towards men', 'War to end all Wars', 'A land fit for heroes to live in', 'Join the Army, and save the World', this sort of claptrap always gets me on the 'raw', because they don't mean half that they say. To talk about the sanctity of human life, and love our neighbour as thyself, when at the same time they are encouraging every effort to produce more powerful and terrible methods of destruction, is nothing else but rank hypocrisy.

The conference table is the proper place to settle disputes, and in my opinion, if the United States of America, Great Britain, and the Soviet Union, would rid themselves of the idea that they can dictate to the world, and make other countries conform to their way of thinking, there would be more peace and a lot more goodwill.

It is high time, too, that Great Britain got rid of the antiquated Victorian attitude, that it is necessary for her to police the world, and maintain an immense Army, Navy, and Air Force. In order to do so, the cost only cripples the financial resources of the countries, but also takes the young virile men of the nation, just when they are needed in industry. However, these things happen to everyone, and have to be faced up to.

Chapter 39

Tommy was now coming along well, he was a bonny little chap, Norah was very proud of him and looking forward to the time when Oliver, her husband, would be able to see him. But all her hopes were dashed to the ground.

Tommy Betteridge, 1943

The London Irish Rifles were moved to Sicily and put into training, very intensive, to prepare them for landing in Italy. Oliver was promoted to Company Sergeant Major, and the company took part in the landings on the Anzio bridgehead. The Germans allowed them all to land and get settled in a few miles from the coast. After a few days, they closed in all round the small British force, and shelled them night and day, and there was no chance to retaliate, or Air Force to protect them. Oliver was killed instantaneously by the effects of blast, and another young life was sacrificed to satisfy the demands of international jealousy, and armament manufacturers.

This Anzio landing was in February 1944, and in my opinion, was one of Winston Churchill's blunders, and on a par with his plan for the Gallipoli landing, in the First World War. Full cover ought to have been provided at Anzio by warships, and a strong Air Force. It is easy to plan on paper, but the human element has to face the danger and the slaughter.

This tragic event upset Norah very much, and made her feel very bitter for a very long time, which was understandable, as Oliver had never seen Tommy, except of course on the photographs that Norah sent to him. We all felt the loss very much, but it is a big problem, at any of these terrible times, to express your sympathy in such a way that it does not do more harm than good. Only time will heal the sting, and make life more bearable, while memories of happy times spent together in former years help compensate, to a certain extent, but never satisfy.

Report in The Midland Counties Tribune, March 3rd 1944.

NUNEATON N.C.O. KILLED IN ITALY.

Former Employee of Messrs. J. C. Smiths'.

Mrs. Norah Betteridge, daughter of Mr. and Mrs. Clarke, of 183, College Street, Coton, has received official news from the War Office that her husband, Company Quartermaster Sergt. Oliver Betteridge, has been killed whilst serving with the Forces in Italy.

C.Q.M.S. Oliver Betteridge.

Twenty-eight years of age, Company Quartermaster Sergt. Betteridge was the only son of Mrs. Betteridge, of 289, Edward Street, Nuneaton, and the late Mr. Oliver Betteridge, before joining the Forces in July, 1940, was a popular employee of Messrs. J. C. Smiths-on-the-Bridge, being in the gentlemen's outfitting department. The news of his death has come as a shock to his many friends.

In addition to his wife, deceased is survived by one child, a baby son, Tommy, whom his father had never seen.

Mrs. Oliver Betteridge's father was formerly the licensee of the King William IV. Inn, Coton Road, Nuneaton.

I made a vow, when we definitely knew that Oliver had 'passed on', that I would do all that I possibly could for both of them, Norah and Tommy, to make up in some way for their loss, and try to provide Tommy with some of the things, which I knew Oliver would have obtained for him.

Norah with Tommy, 1944

My Little Lady and I went to Coventry one day, and went to the Hippodrome in the afternoon. After the performance we went and had tea, and then decided to call and see a friend of ours whose husband had obtained a position as manager of a rather large public house. When we went in, Mrs. - was all teeth and smiles, made us very welcome and said to me, "You never expected to find us in a big place like this, did you George, I'll bet it surprised you?" We had a drink together, and then her husband came and had a few words with us.

I watched him closely and weighed him up. I knew some of his past record, and I thought to myself, poor Mrs. -, if my intuition is right, I didn't expect to find them in such a big place, but he won't be long before he is out. He looked worried to death, and he was a bundle of nerves, shaking and jumpy, and seemed to me as if he was expecting trouble, or something to happen. My judgement was right, a couple of weeks later, when the stocktakers came, the cash, and the stock was a lot short, they were turned out, and had to sell a lot of their possessions to keep Mr. - from being sent to jail.

How they finished up or where they went, we never knew, but Mrs. - had pulled him out of trouble several times before, so I guess she would get him on his feet again.

One of the chargehands of the factory came into the office one morning, sat down, and said, "George, don't spread this about, I have been told to keep this a secret, but I can trust you. A friend of mine, a big transport contractor, told me that he and some other contractors were transporting all material from the bomb sites to a place on the coast of the English Channel." I said to him, "Well, there's no need for secrecy about that, what are they taking it all that way for?" He replied, "That's just it, they're going to fill the channel up, and make a road across, so that the Army and all the equipment can be got into France." I had a good laugh to myself afterwards, the tale was so fantastic, but some time later, when the enormous floating landing stage was constructed and towed to the French beach for the landing on D-Day, I knew for what purpose the rubble had been transported.

When the armies had landed in France on June 6, 1944, and the Russian Army had started the long journey towards Germany, the Air Force was developing the Bomber Command, and the type of engine that was being made at our factory was not so much in demand.

Redundancy started in the autumn of 1944, and the number of operators was reduced, gradually, as the orders were completed. In December, my name was on the list, but I saw the Assistant Manager, and he arranged things so that I worked right into the middle of January 1945, before I finished working at the Shadow Factory.

The first man that I went to see was Mr. Jones, the Secretary and District Organiser of the Transport and General Workers Union. We had a good talk, and he advised me to go to Carbodies, they were needing time and record clerks. He said it was a very poor place for wages, but that it would do for a time, while I looked round for something better. I went to the offices and had an interview with Mr G., the Chief Accountant. He fixed me up, and I started work the next day. The work was a bit complicated, but with a bit of tuition, I soon got the hang of the job.

Actually, I was a bit slow at first, but one morning, when five or six were waiting for their work to be recorded, I heard one of them say, "The old bugger's too slow, we shall be all morning, he wants to liven up." When he came the next time, he was on his own, so I called him into the office and said, "<u>Now</u>, tell me what you told the other chaps." He started to bluster, and said he didn't mean anything. Then I told him, "When I have had two or three days, I'll get you away quick enough, but don't make any more wisecracks, or else I'll knock your bloody teeth down your throat." He was always very helpful after this, and we became good friends, in fact, before I had been there very long, I had made friends of nearly all the men and women who were working on the section. The wages were very poor, the only good thing about the job was the fact it was close to the railway station, and also, nobody interfered with you. If your work was correct, you were your own boss.

When the Chief Accountant got to know me, and the quality and accuracy of my work, he started to increase the number of men for me to record. One day when he came to see me, he looked round and said, "Good Morning, Mr. Clarke, how are you going on in here?" I replied, "Alright, thank you, Mr. G., but it's getting very hot and a bit uncomfortable." He looked puzzled, and said, "Hot, I don't think it's hot, the atmosphere seems just right to me." I replied, "I don't mean atmospheric heat, I mean the pace, if you keep increasing the number that I have got to record, I shall soon be looking after half the operators in the factory." He smiled and said, "Well, you <u>know</u> you can do it, and I know you can." I replied, "When I came here, the job was alright, but the wages are terribly poor, and I don't intend to work myself to death for a lower rate of pay than factory labourers." He said, "Alright, I won't send any more to you."

The railway station was quite close to the factory, but there was a waste piece of land which had to be crossed to get into the factory yard. This was about six inches deep in mud and slush. Men, and quite a number of women, had to walk through this twice a day, all of them grumbling and growling. I mentioned this matter to the Shop Steward, but he said that he couldn't do anything about it.

When I went into the main office the next day to get my office key, the Chief Accountant was there, so I said, "Good morning, Mr. G., your boots are nice and clean, look at mine." He replied, "My word, they are in a mess." I told him, "Yes, and so are all boots and shoes of the men and women who come into the factory that way. Have you had a look around there lately, it's a disgrace, a good path could be made with two or three lorry loads of ashes, and you've got plenty of those." He promised to have a look and get something done.

A week went by, nothing was done, and walking across one morning, I slipped on some bricks that someone had put up for stepping stones, and the bottom of my best overcoat, in addition to my boots, were plastered with mud and slime.

The Chief Accountant was in his usual seat of judgement, so I went up to him, pointed to my coat and boots, and said, "Nothing has been done, look at this bloody mess, and a few loads of ashes will alter everything, I wonder that the women come through it, their feet must get wet." He said that he was sorry, and that he would have something done to make things better. When we went home that night, a good cinder path had been made right up to the main road. This incident shows that a bit of common sense and straight talk can get things done, and others put right. It's no use letting off steam, when nobody concerned, or who should be able to rectify the matter, is not present, the Shop Steward, or a deputation of the workers, could have had the same thing done, that came about through my efforts, but they lacked the guts.

Carbodies, as the name implies, started in a very small way making panel work and bodies for cars and lorries. The firm was a family one in the first year or two, but it succeeded so well, and expanded so much, that a Company was formed, and during the War years, they had some very big Government contracts for varied sheet metal goods.

The noise in the factory was terrific, enormous big presses were grinding and crashing, panel beaters were hammering away, and the old-fashioned iron wheeled trucks were rattling along the concrete gangways all the time, bringing and taking the material and sheet metal from section to section.

As the day crept on, and the factory got darker, one large section, where acetylene welding was being done, it reminded me of a description of Dante's Inferno that I had read about some time or other. The lights kept flashing up, all colours and sizes, outlining the workmen, who looked like inhabitants of another world with their protective masks on. I didn't really dislike the place, but the wage was very poor, so I wrote to one of our local firms for a position on their staff. They had no vacancy at the time, but informed me that they would let me know when anything suitable came along. This materialised, unexpectedly, later on in the year.

It was one of the meanest firms that I ever worked for, and they were dead sure on clocking in and out times, one minute past the quarter hour time, and that quarter was stopped from your wages. They were just as keen on overtime payments, no matter how much you obliged them. About half of the time clerks were women, who were working spare time, about five half days per week, for very poor pay.

The weather was very bad during the first part of the year, and at the end of March, the heat was cut off from the factory and the offices were very cold first thing in the morning. The women time clerks grumbled about this, and one of them wrote out a protest list which we all signed, and then it was taken to the Works Manager, who ignored it. We all talked the matter over the next day, and decided to stay out the same afternoon, in order to get something done about the matter. We also decided to see the Chief Fuel Overseer in Coventry, to obtain his consent to the factory offices to be kept heated until the weather altered. We met in the small park in Grey Friars Green, the sun came out, and the weather was lovely, two of the women went to see the Fuel Officer, and we all felt like a pack of silly buggers, the weather had changed, and it was very warm. Needless to say, the Fuel Officer laughed at the deputation, and turned the enquiry down.

When we turned up for work the next morning, the women, who were working spare time, said that Mr. G. had called round at their homes the previous night, paid them up, and dismissed them. He was waiting at the Gateman's Office for all the full time clerks, and had one in at a time, and those who wanted to restart had to sign a new agreement, which one or two did and started again. Five or more of us were fed up and packed the job up, when it came to my turn, I replied, "No, thank you, Mr. G., this is the worst firm that I have ever worked for, I've been fed up for some time, so I'll have my cards and finish, there are no prospects here."

That was the last job that I had in Coventry, and I had no desire to get another one there. When I got home, my Little Lady looked at me, and said, "What's the matter, George, you're home early, aren't you well?" I replied, "I'm all right, my dear, but you needn't put me any more sandwiches up for a day or two, I'm finished at Carbodies."

I went down to the Labour Exchange the next day, signed on, and was then placed on the list of disabled men ready for work. After a few days, the clerk in charge told me to go to a new building estate close to where I lived; Tarmac Ltd. were going to make the roads, and required one or two clerks. I went there, and met the clerk in charge and he said that I was just the right man for the position, but that the agent set everybody on. The agent came, asked me one or two particulars, then he said, "You'll do, how much money do you want?" I replied, "Well, I've been getting five pounds a week plus overtime at my last place." He said, "Right, five quid a week, if we don't like you we shall sack you, and if you don't like us, you can leave any time you like to."

Naturally, I was pleased to have got fixed up so quickly, especially as large numbers of men were being made redundant and were signing on at the Labour Exchange.

When I was getting ready for work the next morning, the postman came, and one of the letters was from the firm that I had applied for a position, several weeks previous. The manager, Mr. A. K. Barby, informed me that there was a vacancy which he thought would suit me, and would I call and see him.

When I got to my work on the development estate, I asked the charge hand for an hour off, and got on the phone to Mr. Barby. He told me that the job was in the Cashier's Department to help with the records, timekeeping, and wages. I told him that I had just been fixed up, but if terms were alright, I would rather work in this firm as the conditions would be more suitable. He asked me what wage 1 would accept and I told them that Tarmac Ltd were going to pay me five pounds per week and overtime. Mr. Barby said that he could only offer me four pounds per week, two weeks holiday with pay, and wages paid if off through illness, etc., I said I would think it over, and let him know by the first post the next day.

When I told my Little Lady she begged me to accept the offer, and my daughters backed her up. I told her that it would mean a pound a week less for her, but she said, "Take the job, never mind the money, we'll manage somehow."

Chapter 40

I commenced work at Messrs. J. Ellis & Sons Ltd[42] at their branch office at Hinckley in May, 1945. Mr A.K. Barby was the District Manager, and for more than five years I worked under him, and enjoyed this period of employment more than any that I had had for many years. The travelling to and from work was very handy, the hours were good, working conditions very pleasant and comfortable, and the staff were very friendly.

The firm was a very old established one, obliging, fair, but firm in all its dealings with all its customers, who covered a wide area of Leicestershire, Warwickshire, Northants, and Rutland. Farm produce was bought and sold, farmers were supplied with all their requirements, builders with all that they needed, bricks, stones, sand, cement, paint etc. In addition, the firm ran a large transport service, and had coal and coke supply depots all over the surrounding districts.

The Office Manager and Cashier was a young man named Frank Thistlethwaite, and we got on very well together. He knew that he could trust me, we were both conscientious workers, and well on top of our work, which counts very much in a busy office. Mr. Barby was a good manager, pleasant and courteous, never grumbled or found fault without good reasons, but when things went wrong he could be firm, and make things hum a bit. He had a very good name with most of the farmers, who knew that they could rely on him to give them a square deal, whatever the goods he supplied them with, or bought off them.

My work consisted of timekeeping, wages, income tax, and keeping records of the intake of wheat, barley, oats, straw, hay, etc., also recording the supplies of lime, chalk

---

[42] *They later became Ellis and Everard, Agricultural Merchants.*

and other bulk fertilisers, and making certificates out for the same material so that the farmers could obtain the Government subsidy, which at that time was 50% of the total cost, a very great help to the farmer.

In August 1945, on the 15th, the German Army capitulated, then the great struggle began to get things straightened out and get on an even keel again, after all the senseless destruction which ought to have been prevented by firmer dealings with Germany after the first World War.

Celebrations were held all over the world. Street parties were held in all the cities, towns, and villages in Great Britain, but over all the celebrations there was the shadow and memories of some dear ones, who had paid the price of Victory, by death from bombs, etc. Almost as soon as the War was over, Winston Churchill turned round on his Labour colleagues, who had done everything in their power to help and assist him. He also put the "breeze up" Stalin and the Soviet Government.

He went to the Country, and in the Election, the Tories got the worst defeat that they had ever had. The Labour Party swept the country, and were successful by a very large majority. Winston had the shock of his career, he had the idea that his own popularity and personality would sway public opinion, but the ordinary people had had enough of Toryism, for a time, anyhow, and Winston was defeated and deflated.

At that time I was about the only one in the Office with strong Labour views, the other members of the staff were either out and out Tories, or Liberals, or neutrals, and as I have never been afraid of expressing my views, I met with a great deal of criticism and opposition when discussing the political situation and national affairs. The Boss and I had some very interesting talks. He was Conservative in outlook, but he was broadminded and always willing to admit that some items of the Labour Government policy would be beneficial to the country, if they materialised. Hinckley and the district roundabout was a Tory stronghold, and Labour men were classed as "Reds." When the Labour Government, with Mr. Atlee as Prime Minister, started with some of the reforms which were included in their programme, the general outcry of the national newspapers was that everybody would be ruined, the country would go into bankruptcy, and unemployment would be the lot of the working population.

What a shock it was with them, and the Tory Party, when the policy of the Labour Party succeeded beyond all expectations. The way in which the ex-service men were looked after and fixed up, either in their old jobs, or as trainees in different trades and professions, with something entirely different to the way in which they were treated by the Tories after the first World War.

Mistakes and blunders were made, of course, but they were the result of too much eagerness, and trying to do too many things at once, but they were young, and the young always try to run before they can walk, which is a bad practice when time is limited. Errors cannot be rectified, nor blunders put right, in the short period of the statutory time of a Government, before the wolves of the national press, and the general outcry of public opinion, backed up by the capitalists, demands someone's head on a charger, and often a good man packs up in disgust. The general population of Britain is very fickle, and easily swayed by big headlines, bombastic leading articles, and fault finding by experts in propaganda and sensationalism.

Two of the biggest mistakes that the Labour Government made, were, in my opinion:

271

1. the granting of the five day week to the miners was much too soon; I am an old experienced miner, and the miners would have carried on and worked on Sundays as well, until the stocks of coal were built up, if the position of the country's needs had been properly explained, and their wages increased by a considerable amount
2. the Ground Nut Scheme[43] was started before they had the proper mechanical equipment suitable for such a rough stretch of country, the surface of which, quite a large proportion, was unsuitable.

For all their mistakes and excessive eagerness, (many of their plans and schemes ought to have been curbed, and held in abeyance, until some of the main objects had been consolidated), the Labour Government did more for the working classes in the short period that they were in power, than other parties had done in the previous fifty years, and all of it accomplished by good planning and legislation, against bitter opposition.

Control of prices and subsidies kept the cost of living at a reasonable and stable level for all sections of the community, and rationing ensured fair shares for all. Nationalisation of the Coal Mining Industry saved this industry from fading away, as the miners were fed up with the private Coal Owner's tactics, wage cutting, conditions in the mines, and the miserable rates of compensation for accidents, injuries, and the totally inadequate amounts paid to widows and dependent children, when fatal accidents caused the loss of the breadwinner.

---

[43] *A project for growing groundnuts, (peanuts), on virgin lands in East Africa to feed the growing populations, and enable the African colonial soldiers who had helped defeat the Italian and German armies in Africa use the earth-moving equipment that had been used in the African campaigns to build roads and airfields.*

Only very good wages, and better conditions, have kept the number of men in the industry at a reasonable level, and no fresh recruits would have entered the mines on the pre war treatment. The Social Services, Health, Hospital, Optical, and Ambulance facilities are something for Britain to be proud of, and providing the Tory Government does not sabotage these, they will be in the future, the envy of the world.

When the country settled down to work again, after the defeat of the Conservatives, the working population had the most regular and stable employment period that they have ever known, and instead of showing their appreciation, the Unions harassed the Government by their claims and demands, most of them very unfair. The claims were all met as far as possible, in a very fair way, but this still did not satisfy their greed, and they could not see that their actions were doing immense harm to the Labour Party.

As the men were being discharged from the Army, we had four or five young men come to work in the Hinckley offices, and one day they were in my office, comparing their rate of pay with that of the miners, running Nationalisation down, and calling the miners idle, good for nothing, and dissolute. I listened to them for some time, and then I asked them if they had ever done any really hard work. They all replied that they had worked very hard in the Army, for very little money.

I said, "Now, my lads, I had twenty years in the mines, and I know what hard work is, when you work until the sweat runs into your boots, and you are almost too tired to walk home, your legs, your back, and your muscles ache, and when you do land home, you could almost empty the water tap to quench your thirst, that's what hard work is, and it is the miner's daily task. Another thing, there's plenty of jobs for all of you in the mines, and good wages, but don't forget you've <u>got</u> to work, if you want to get on."

The winter of 1946 began with some terribly bad weather, which continued right through into March 1947, and the coal stocks of the country, which were at a very low level at the beginning of the bad weather, were further depleted through transport difficulties, caused by the heavy snowfalls, frost etc., which made the roads bad for heavy portage, and also caused a terrible amount of trouble on the railways. Of course, according to the National Tory papers, this was all the fault of the Labour Government.

One of our lorry drivers, a new man, went out to an outlying farm about eight miles from Hinckley, with a load of feeding stuff, and then reloaded with stock feed potatoes. On the farm road he got stuck in the heavy snow and slush, and it was snowing heavily. Instead of getting on to the nearest phone and asking for another lorry to come and pull him out, he came right back to the depot, and reported there. Mr. Barby, the lorry driver, and three more men went in a lorry to the breakdown, and they had a job to find the lorry, the snowfall had been terrific, the wind had also caused big drifts, the men had to dig a road up to the buried lorry, then dig it out, and tow it back to Hinckley.

The air was 'blue' with the language, the men were blue with cold, and that poor lorry driver went through the mill, he wouldn't forget that lesson, nor the trouble, caused by his inexperience.

The same year, two or three German prisoners of war came to work in the yard, and help in the store sheds. They were big strong men, very pleasant and obliging, willing, and very good workers. The wages that they earned were paid to the Committee, who fixed up all the working arrangements, and allowed the men pocket money. The men were transported from the prisoners of war camp, in the morning, and taken back at night.

I travelled back to Nuneaton in the same car, two or three times every week, it was on the route to the camp, and several times I went there, and had a look round for a few minutes. It was situated in Arbury Park, well away from any houses and main roads It was a rather large camp, consisting of wooden huts enclosed by a very high, strong wire fence, and there was a company of British soldiers to guard all roads to the camp, and of course, the prisoners as well.

The men who work at our place at Hinckley talked to me quite a lot about Germany, and their war experience. They, nor the ordinary working class people, had no desire for war or army life, what they wanted was a good job, good wages, and the pleasant home life. On Friday nights, I always treated them to chips, and when we were in the car on Fridays, they would say, "Mistur Clarke, chips tonight, very good, thank you very much." One of the main questions that they used to ask me was, "When you think we go back home to Germany, Mistur Clark, our wives and children are waiting for us, do you think it will be soon?"

My wages had now been increased to a more reasonable amount, the members of the staff were all very friendly, the office was very comfortable, and although at times the work increased, I was always able to keep on top.

Chapter 41

During the five years that I was at Ellis & Sons, I had the most peaceful job of my life. In other jobs, I had earned much bigger wages, but I had to work very hard and worry as well, and there was always the feeling that it would not last.

Gertie, late 1940s

We were very happy and contented at home, though it was still very trying for the housewives, trying enough to put on the table at meal times, and my Little Lady went to a lot of trouble to try and get something tasty and nourishing. The rations allowed were still very meagre, but there was plenty of bread, potatoes, and other vegetables, so we had plenty of very plain food, helped out by spam, jam, and marmalade. My wife became quite an expert carver, she cut slices off the Sunday joint as thin as tissue paper.

In the autumn of 1949, my health began to worry me slightly. I felt very tired, my legs ached very badly, and I became irritable, and easily depressed. I tried my usual tonic, which had always put me right in previous years, but this time it had no good effect, and I got no better. I went to see my doctor, he told me that I was much too heavy and needed a good rest. After two or three weeks at home, he advised me to see a specialist, who gave me a check up, and advised me to go on a very plain diet. I started work again, kept on a diet, and lost twelve pounds in about ten days.

I worked up to the Christmas of 1949, and when I was in the bus travelling to Hinckley after the holidays, I had a very queer feeling come over me; when I landed at the offices, I went to mine, took my coat off and sat down. I lit a cigarette, started to cough, the perspiration streaming from my head and ran down my face, I went very cold, and then collapsed.

When I came round, I heard Mr. Barby say to Frank, the office manager, "I think this is it, Frank." I looked at them, and said, "What happened, how long have I been like this?" Mr. Barby replied, "Sit still, old man, keep quiet and don't worry yourself, we have sent for the doctor." When the doctor came he questioned me, and then checked up with his stethoscope, he said that I must go home as soon as possible, that he would send the ambulance to take me and that I must get to bed, and send for my own doctor at once.

The boss came to see me when the ambulance came, and he said, "Now, don't worry over anything at all, have a good rest, you can come back when you're ready, there's a job here for you as long as you want one, so long, old man, and good luck." I got the ambulance driver to pull up at my doctor's surgery. He questioned me, and then told me to go home, get to bed, and then he would call later. When I reached home, Frank and Winnie, one of the office staff, had been over in the car to let my Little Lady know, so that it would not be too great a shock, and Winnie was staying with her.

I walked from the ambulance into the house, my Little Lady smiled at me, help me off with my coat jacket, and said, "Come on now, old man, let's get you into bed, that's what you need." Winnie said, "At least, you're still on your feet, take care of yourself, we shall all be thinking about you at the office, I will tell them when I get back."

When I got into the warm bed, it was like Heaven, and after a good hot drink I went to sleep. Later on in the morning the doctor came, checked up and examined me all over, then gave me some tablets, and told me to get as much sleep as possible. The first night I was rather restless, and pains in my chest made me feel uneasy and rather anxious. When the doctor came the next day, I told them about it, and he said that they would pass, I was not to worry.

After two or three days I felt a lot better, and was able to be propped up a bit in bed, so that I could read until I was tired, and then go to sleep. When I had been in bed about a week, and taken an enormous number of tablets, all sorts, colours, and sizes, I asked the doctor when he thought I would be ready to go back to work again. He looked at me, and with a twinkle in his eyes, said, "Mr. Clarke, you're a very lucky man to be here at all considering what you have had, work is out of the question for a long time. I'm your boss now, and you must stay in bed at least six weeks, perhaps longer, and then you will require a long rest, and take things very easy."

It was a severe attack of Coronary Thrombosis that had caused my collapse, and I knew from what I had read and been told about this complaint that only a long period of quiet rest would enable me to resume my normal life again.

I made myself contented, read all sorts of books as well as the daily papers, sorted some winners (?) out, had a bob or two on, and slept the rest of the time. My Little Lady nursed me, and looked after me like any really good professional nurse would have done, but in addition there was her affection, calm, and patience, nothing was too much trouble when my comfort and wishes were concerned.

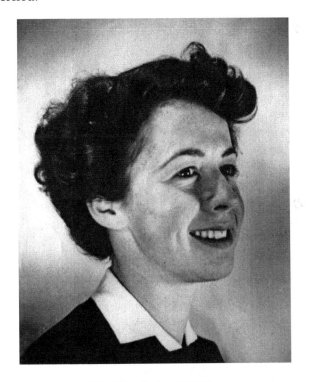

Mollie, late 1940s

My daughters, Norah, Mollie, and Audrey, were all very considerate and helpful, keeping me supplied with books from the Library and elsewhere. Tommy, my grandson, was also very helpful. As soon as he came in from school, he would come upstairs to see if I wanted anything, and usually brought a fresh hot water bottle, as the weather was very cold at this time.

After about six weeks, the doctor told me that I could get up, and sit in the bedroom a short time each day, and my legs began to get stronger, so that I could walk around the room better, and more often, each day.

Mr. Barby and the office staff were very kind and considerate, and the firm paid me my wages in full for more than four months, which kindness I shall never forget, and I only regret that I was unable to resume work again, in order to repay them, by good service, for their consideration.

One word about the firm, the original founders of the company were Quakers, and I think that most of the present directors are also Quakers, and every company that was founded and run by such men is noted for its consideration and human feelings towards their staff and employees. Cadburys, Rowntrees, Fry's and numerous other good firms were all founded by Quakers.

As I got stronger, and a bit steadier on my legs, it made things a bit easier for my wife, as she did not have to come upstairs so many times, and I often waited, if possible, until Tommy, or the girls came in, before asking for anything.

One dinner time, when Tommy came home from school, he came upstairs to see me, to see whether I wanted anything. He was laughing, and said, "Watch your step, Grand-Dad, the old gel's on the warpath again, she's been running me round." He was just at that age, then, when lads are full of fun and mischief, that is, if they are real lads.

I came downstairs for the first time after about three months. It was quite a change, and I was able to get round the house from room to room with the aid of a good walking stick, and steadying myself on the furniture. After some weeks, I was able to get round the garden, and also down to the front gate, which made a welcome change from being indoors, and I was able to have a talk to my friends. I asked my doctor, when he called to see me one day, whether I had better let my employers know that it would be a long time before I would be able to return to work, and he told me that my boss had been on the phone, and asked the same question, and that he had told him that it would be several months before he consented to let me start again.

I asked him then, "Do you think it will be possible then, or do you think it best for me to give up the idea of starting again, and perhaps avoid another collapse?" He replied, "Mr. Clarke, if I was in your place, I would give up the idea of going out to work, take things easy, and make yourself contented with what you have got. It will be better for you, and your wife, and in addition, you will enjoy life a lot longer."

I let the firm know, and received a cheque from them as well as a nice letter from Mr. Barby, in which he told me that if I wanted a job in the future, he would always find one for me. Thus ended my actual working life, and as my daughters were living with us, my Little Lady was able, with their help, financially and in many other ways, to keep the budget balanced.

Apart from one or two minor incidents, life went along fairly smoothly. I gave up smoking, and became almost a total abstainer, only having a drop of something or other to celebrate special occasion. I had one or two falls, and broke my arm badly on one occasion, but I got over it and am still able to do odd jobs around the house and in the garden, when members of my family will let me, so that on the whole, I have got nothing to complain about.

Chapter 42

Well, now we are in the year of 1950, and owing to goods, especially the main essentials for the table, being in short supply, rationing was still in force to ensure fair shares, while subsidies and price controls kept the cost of living at a fair level for the lower paid workers, and the old aged pensioners.

As the statutory period of the Labour Government was now drawing to a close, the Conservatives started to prepare for the General Election, by clever propaganda work of a large team of experts, led and managed by Lord Woolton and Lord Beaverbrook. This, and the publicity in the national Tory Press, influenced the gullible voters, especially the female section, and they forgot all about the benefits and improvements in their working and living conditions which had come about through the efforts of the Labour Party, and the Labour Government.

When the Election had taken place, the Tories were successful by a very small majority, and when they got settled in, were very careful not to upset the working population too much, as the two parties were nearly equal in number, and the small Liberal vote could have brought the downfall of the Government about, if the Tory Party leaders had allowed any slack attendance.

During their period of office, they enjoyed the fruits of Labour's enterprise, and soft soaped the majority of the workers so cleverly that they got the credit for full employment, good wages, and social services, which would never have been made possible by Conservative methods and obsolete ideas, had they been in power, after the second World War.

Their methods and ideas were very much in evidence after the first World War, and for a period of fifteen years, Britain was in a very poor way, millions out of work, living standards very low, shops full of foodstuffs, clothing, boots and shoes, furniture, etc etc., and no money to purchase them. The pawn shops, the bob a week tallymen, the county court judges, and the bailiffs, were busy. But many small traders and shopkeepers were ruined.

In 1953, my Little Lady had a very severe attack of neuritis and lumbago, and for several weeks this was a big handicap for her, we all had to buckle to and help her as much as we could. In time, this troubled passed, and she was once more like her old self again, though her legs ached very much at times and she would not have two or three days complete rest, which we all told her she needed.

Norah and Tommy had lived with us until Tommy was 12 years old, when Norah got married again to a very nice man, a widower with three grown-up children, and a very nice home.[44]

Following Norah's second marriage in 1954, Audrey was married in December 1954, to a very nice Irish man, named Thomas Sheehan[45], they both came to live with us, and we were all very happy together. This was our third Tommy to keep us company, and my wife was very fond of him.

Tommy is now, at the time I am writing this, nearly 14 years of age, a very good intelligent lad, full of fun and

---

[44] *Norah's second husband was Harry James Sidwell, born 1915, who lived at 53, Marston Lane in Attleborough. Harry taught at Caldwell Junior School, and was later Head at Galley Common Infants School. He died in 1999. The male Sidwell line in Nuneaton is clearly documented back to 1828, and with one possible link yet to be confirmed, to the Robert Sidwell who married a Mary in Nuneaton in 1661 in St. Nicholas Parish Church, and had four children baptised there. But that's another story.*

[45] *Family legend says she chose him because he looked like Gregory Peck.*

energy, fond of games, sport, and reading, and also very considerate, thoughtful, and devoted to his mother.[46]

Tommy Betteridge with Gertie, 1955

---

[46] *Tom used to walk home to College Street from Shepperton Junior School through Chilvers Coton Churchyard. In his own words "...there was a very rough gang who gave all the other kids a very torrid time...they were particularly adept at taking flowers from the graves and beating kids around the head with them – chrysanths were the worst – and I don't think I ever recovered from being dropped into an empty grave !"*

Tommy now has got a little brother, a grand little chap, to help look after, and perhaps in later life, to protect and guide through the battle of life.

George, Norah and David, early 1956

Everything was going all right during the first few months of 1955, but then my wife's health began to fail. Her appetite had always been very good, and there was no doubt that partaking of good food in reasonable quantities helped her to keep her energy, good spirits, and vivacity. In the middle of the year her appetite began to get worse and worse, and she lost weight very rapidly. Our family doctor could not properly get to the cause of the trouble, and advised her to see a specialist at our own local hospital. After two or three visits, and very thorough checkups, he said that it was a case of severe anaemia, and that my Little Lady would have to attend the out-patients clinic for injections.

She was also taking a well-known remedy for nervous debility, and run down condition, at home. I am sure this did cause a wonderful amount of improvement to her general health, coupled with hospital treatment. In a few weeks, she began to put on weight again, recovered her appetite, and looked like her old self again, charming and pleasant. I did all that I could to make her take life more easily, some days she would do so, and then at other times do too much, and tire herself out.

Her birthday came along on September 29, 1955, sixty eight years, a lifetime of love, patience, and helpfulness. I often thought as I sat and looked at her without her knowing when we were alone together some nights, how lovely, happy, and contented she looked when she was sewing, darning, reading, or balancing the budget.

My birthday came along November the 18th, and I had reached my three score years and 10, seventy years of toil, turmoil, love, sorrow, patience, tolerance, but also a certain amount of rebelliousness against injustice and class distinction.

I remember one episode when I was at Hinckley, Mr. Barby, accompanied by two of the three directors of the firm, came through to my office, and when they got to my desk, Mr. Barby said, "This is Mr. Clarke, our pet red, he has got a grievance against the world." I looked up at them, and replied, "Good morning, gentlemen, but, Mr. Barby, don't give them a wrong impression of me, my grievance is not against the world, only against the way it is being run." One of the directors said, "That's quite right, Mr. Clarke, carry on with the good work."

As the end of the year came nearer and nearer, I began to think that we were really going to enjoy life and have a good time at Christmas. With all the members of the family things seemed to be more settled, and I thought that we were in for a spell of good luck, which we both needed. But fate stepped in again, and dealt me the worst blow that I have ever had.

George and Gertie at 183 College Street, early 1950s

On Sunday, December 4, 1955, we had a very pleasant, enjoyable day and evening, I went to bed first as I usually do every night, and my Little Lady came shortly afterwards. She seemed very happy, and was talking to me until she got into bed. She had a very severe attack of Coronary Thrombosis, and although we got the services of a very good doctor (he lived only a few yards from our house) who came over at once, it was of no avail, my wife faded quietly and peacefully away and 'passed on' to what I sincerely hope is eternal rest. She

288

earned and needed it, like thousands of women do, who have children, and mother them in the right way.

It was a terrible shock to all of us, the only consolation we had was that she did not suffer any severe pain, except for a few minutes, as it was all over in a short space of about 20 minutes, almost unbelievable, at the time it happens.

Now I was on my own except for my daughters, and I had to brace myself up to carry the burden as well as I could, in order not to cause them more anxiety, they were suffering enough from the suddenness and shock of their tragic loss. It was rather strange, but during the previous year or two, my Little Lady had always told me that if anything happened to her, I must always keep my own home, and not live with anyone else. I used to laugh at her, and I told her several times that she would live years longer than me, and perhaps marry again, to a better man.

After two or three weeks, the reaction set in, and I felt very lonely and depressed, but I was very thankful that I did not feel so bitter as I did about the loss of our own son Tom, this had made me hard and resentful with a grievance against everybody and everything, especially motorists and motor cyclists. I wanted now to be on my own, I felt full up with emotion, and a man does not like to let others see him break down, and cry like a child. This passed after a time, and I found comfort in memories of our happy times together.

Now, after more than twelve months, I feel more restful and my mind is more peaceful. I do not think that I have lost my Little Lady altogether, her spirit is still with me all the time, and when any problem presents itself, I always try to solve it in the same way that we did when we were together. Her intuition, influence, inspiration, and sound commonsense stopped me, many a time, from being too hasty, rash, or reckless. Some may think these are the wandering and rambling thoughts of old age, but I do not think so.

I am, at the present time, more mentally alert, and more confident of my own judgement than ever I was in my younger days, and I am more convinced, now, more than ever I was before in my life, that when a person dies, who has loved deeply, and also been loved, the spirit still lives, if only in the memory and thoughts of those who never forget, and never wish to do so.

Chapter 43

Well, now the readers of this book may think what does all this rather disjointed story of my life lead up to, and what useful purpose would it serve.

The first thing I want to impress upon the present working generations, is that the young ones, in their 20s and 30s, and also a large number of the 40s and 50s, are going through life with the mistaken idea that they need not bother themselves over which party is in power,

I've tried to point out the enormous changes in the financial working conditions, social benefits, and standards of living in the working population of Britain (and the working population I mean, are those who, if they do not use their brains, skill, or physical powers, in the production of the real wealth of the rich nation, receive no income) and to make them realise that all this has been brought about by the Labour Party and the Trade Unions, who have had to fight and suffer against very strong, clever, bitter opposition for many years.

I want to do my utmost to get the Labour Party back in power again, so that there will be sound, sensible men in charge of the nation's affairs, who have been through the mill, and know, or ought to know, what is needed to ensure a fair share of the world's bounteous produce for everyone, instead of the present state of affairs whereby those who never do a day's work from the day of their birth till they die, get all and everything they desire, and live in luxury all their lives.

Another problem that will only be solved by a strong, united Labour Government, is the Old Aged Pensioners welfare. The Conservatives are always promising better treatment, but promises are no good when they are not fulfilled, and have never showed any feeling of consideration for the aged and infirm, until they were compelled by the insistent efforts of the Labour Party and the Trade Unions.

This is what the present working population must never forget, and a good substantial pension scheme must be made compulsory, so that everyone is assured of a comfortable living when they finish work, and can claim it as their right, and in that way retain their feeling of independence and contentment.

If only the Trade Unions and all the workers of this great nation of ours would only have the sense to drop their wage claims for a time, and use their enormous power to compel the Government to bring this plan into force, it can be done.

What everyone must realise, is that the 'don't care a damn' attitude, 'bugger you, Jack, I'm all right', does not get anywhere, but we all get old and infirm some time, and if old people are sure of a really good income, it goes a good way to ensure their happiness and contentment, for the last years of their lives, and they are entitled to that, most of them, anyhow.

I want to see a good strong Labour Government revise the system of taxation, which needs thoroughly overhauling, in order to make those who have such large shares of the nation's currency pay their fair proportion, and not be able to evade such payments by the aid of clever, unscrupulous, and corrupt accountants, solicitors, and many others.

What I think about the system of taxation would take too much space to explain, but just one or two paragraphs to show what I will call the "Roundabout", I had a year or two as a P.A.Y.E. Clerk.

The worker, man or woman, who pays income tax on the P.A.Y.E. system, has every penny that is due stopped from his or her wages every pay day. When they spend their money at the shops, pubs, theatres, cinemas, other places, they pay direct tax, purchase tax, excise tax, entertainment tax, and many others. They cannot evade them, they have to pay. In addition, they have to pay indirectly (on the price of the goods, articles, or entrance fees), the income tax of the firms, proprietors, managers and employees, which is added to the cost price in addition to the normal profit margin.

If I was in charge of the Income Tax Department, I would devise some means whereby those firms, grossly overpaid professional people, and entertainment stars, would have to pay much more than they do, and pay it in full every three months. I would not give them the chance to carry on for two or three years without paying anything, live in the lap of luxury, spending all they can get hold of, and then going bankrupt to clear themselves.

What Great Britain needs very badly at the present time and for future years, is sound, sensible, clearheaded government, by men who will come down to earth, consolidate our position in world affairs, and stop interfering with other countries. There is plenty of work to be done to put our own home and Commonwealth affairs in good order, instead of trying to police the world, and make other countries govern, and rule, the people according to the standards we desire, coupled with those of the U.S.A.

The scandalous waste of the national income on crack-brained ideas, like rockets and space ships, jet planes, and air liners travelling at terrific speeds, H bombs, A bombs, and all such lunacy ought to be cut out, and the labour and money used to serve a more useful purpose, so that this in time would benefit the taxpayers in two ways, i.e. taxation could be greatly reduced, and the money and labour employed on something worthwhile to benefit everybody, not for mad destruction.

I could carry on for hours, but the main purpose of my statements is to try and make the young people realise that there is much more in life than Rock and Roll, Jazz, Tin Pan Alley music, speeding through life so fast that they haven't got time for clear thinking, and attention to things that really bring enjoyment, contentment, and happiness.

Another matter that requires attention is the money that is squandered on crooners, moaners, females who are not afraid to flaunt their bare bodies, and make excessive sex appeal their chief attraction. I have always loved women, and have been attracted by their charm and physical qualities, but I do like some delicate restraint, and not have sex exhibitions like uncivilised savages. Also, most decent people are fed up with the regular daily display of sexy women in the papers.

Now, I'm getting ready for the close of the story of my life, but I hope that I shall live many more years, and who knows, perhaps some of my ideals will materialise. Nothing would give me more pleasure if they did, and as I have stated before, improvements can only come about by the united efforts of the working classes.

If I am fortunate enough to get this life story published, and I am able to afford it, I want to make a caravan tour round the villages and beauty spots in Britain, talk to some of the people, and get to know their views, their outlook on life, and its everyday problems. Then, if I am still able, I would like to travel round the world, not in the air, but on the seas and oceans, there is nothing more enjoyable and health giving than a sea voyage, you get away from the noise, turmoil, and stress.

This has been my ambition all my life, and now, after losing my best pal, my Little Lady, I could go, she never had any desire to go on any caravan tour, or long sea voyages.

At the finish, a few words to young people who are married, or who are contemplating getting married.

Don't rush things too much, weigh everything up well before doing it, be patient, tolerant, truthful, affectionate, and always pull together. Live within your income, and if there is any surplus after putting a little away for emergencies, share the remainder. The world situation, and the position on the home front, looks very black and unpromising at the present time, and in my opinion, only demonstrates how futile and helpless the threat of all-out War, and the use of powerful and destructive bombs, is in the settlement of world problems. These can, and ought to be, settled round the conference table, and if the USA, Britain, France, the Commonwealth, Russia and her allies, would get together in the right spirit, this can be done.

G. L. Clarke. January 28th, 1957.

Appendix

I want, now that I have completed my story, to give my thanks to some of those without whose help and care I could not have done so.

First, to my daughters, Norah, Mollie, and Audrey, who, since I lost my Little Lady, have all done their best to comfort and console me. They have also looked after my material comforts, kept up my morale, and there is no doubt that their efforts kept me from feeling too depressed, and helped me to carry on again.

Thanks also, to my sons in law, Harry and Tom, who have been very helpful and considerate, without overdoing it and interfering too much.

Also, to my grandson, Tommy, who has always kept in close touch with me every week, and I always look forward to seeing his smiling face whenever he comes to see me.

I also want to thank the trio of doctors, Messrs. Neil, Busby, and Martin, who have looked after the family's health and welfare over the years, especially Dr. Busby, who has looked after me during the past seven years, and taken such a big interest in my well-being, and general health.

Now I want to give a pat on the back, if we can call it that, to the National Health and Hospital services, including the transport and ambulance section.

Some months ago, I had to go into hospital, through an attack of dysentery, and while in there, I was looked after, nursed, fed, and received special treatment from the doctors and they were all grand people, so to the nurses and doctors at the George Eliot and Whitley hospitals, I can only say "Thanks to all of you."

This is all I have got to say, so:

'Don't look for the flaws, as you go through life,

And even if you find 'em,

'Tis wise, and kind, to be somewhat blind

And look to the virtues behind 'em.'

Good wishes, good health, and good luck to everyone, and here's hoping that Labour will come out on top again, and keep there to

THE END

during the past seven years, & taken such a big interest in my well being, & general health. Now I want to give a pat on the back, if we can call it that, to the National Health & Hospital Services, including the Transport & Ambulance Section.

Some months ago, I had to go into hospital, through an attack of dysentry, & while in there, I was looked after, nursed, fed, & received special treatment from the doctors. They were all grand people, So to the nurses & doctors at the George Eliot & Whitley Hospitals, I can only say "Thanks to all of you." This is all I have got to say, So,

"Don't look for the flaws, as you go through life,
And even if you find "em",
Tis wise, & Kind, to be somewhat "blind".
And look for the virtues behind "em"."

Good wishes, good health, & good luck to everyone, & here's hoping, that "Labour" will come out on top again, & keep there to

THE END. (398)

Gertie's mother Eliza Grey, back left, mid 1870s

Eliza, late 1940s

Key dates in George's life

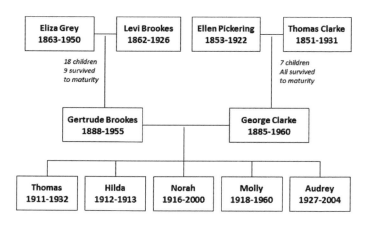

1890   George attends Heath End Infant's School

1896   George attends Shepperton Boy's School

1898   George starts work at Clare Speight Photography Studios on Coton Road. Family moves to Griff Colliery House, Heath End

1900   George moves to engineering shop at Stanley's Brick Works

1901   George travels to South Africa. On returning, he goes back into Stanley's Brickworks, before the family moves to Bilston to take over The Turks Head pub

1902   George's father returns to Newdegate Colliery, moves family back to Bedworth. George works at Newdegate Colliery

1903   George's father moves to Stanley's Colliery, family moves to Grove Road, Stockingford, and then Toler Road. George taken on at Stanley's Colliery

1905   Family moves to rear of Albert's Butcher's Shop in Arbury Road. George starts going to the Drill Hall and meets Gertie

1909   George and Gertie marry on Boxing Day and move into 230 Arbury Road

1910   Tom is born

1912   Hilda is born, and dies of pneumonia in 1913

1914   George, Gertie and Tom move to Denaby, South Yorkshire

1915   George moves to Bullcroft Colliery, and then to Swinton Colliery, and family move to Rawmarsh. Gertie's sister Esther takes tenancy of King William IV pub on Coton Road

1916   Norah is born

1917   George moves back to Newdegate Colliery in Nuneaton, and lives at 26 Arbury Road

1918   Mollie is born. Gertie's parents take over King William

1921   Miner's strike. George out of work for 21 weeks. Ten days after return to work is badly injured in roof fall and spends three months in hospital

1922   After a long recuperation period, George leaves mining after twenty years, and takes over the tenancy of King William from Gertie's parents. George's mother, Ellen, dies aged 69

1927   Audrey is born. The Palace Cinema opens with George's brother Sid as Manager

1928   George and Gertie leave the King William, and open Grocery shop next door on Coton Road

1929   George takes on additional jobs as an usher at the Palace Cinema and as a Debt Collector

1931   Tom joins Coventry Gas Corporation. George's father, Thomas, dies, aged 80

1933   Tom is killed riding his motorcycle

1939   George starts as Steward at Vauxhall Club, and over Christmas is replaced as Steward

1940   George gets a job as Clerk at the Daimler Shadow Factory in Foleshill, and they move into 183 College Street

1940   Norah is married to Oliver Betteridge on November 14th, the night Coventry is blitzed

1941   Air raid on Nuneaton. George's brother Sid is killed, and Chilvers Coton Church suffers a direct hit

1943   Norah's son Thomas Oliver is born

1944   Norah's husband Oliver is killed in Italy

1945   George is made redundant from Daimler, and eventually joins J. Ellis and Sons in Hinckley

1949   George has heart attack and retires

1953   Norah marries for the second time to Harry Sidwell and moves to 53 Marston Lane

1954   Audrey marries Thomas Sheehan, and they live with George at 183 College Street

1955   Gertie dies, aged 67, on Dec 4th

1956   George starts writing his book on July 13th

1957   George finishes the book on Jan 28th

1960   Molly dies on August 13th, aged 42, of leukaemia

1960   George dies, aged 74, on September 18th of peritonitis caused by a perforated duodenal ulcer, and is buried at Chilvers Coton Church, where he and Gertie were married. George was buried on September 22nd in Section B, Row 19, No. 4, into the grave of his son Sidney Thomas Clarke, who was buried there on July 14th 1933.

Postscript

Of George and Gertie's five children, only Norah and Audrey married and had children. Hilda and Thomas died young, and although Mollie died aged 42 (of leukaemia), she never married. Her death saddened George greatly, and he died just over a month later.

However I'm sure George would be pleased to know that at the beginning of 2011, his bloodline lives on through eight great-grandchildren, and four great-great grandchildren:

Norah's first son Thomas (1943-2010) had two daughters, each of whom have two daughters. Her second son David (1956) has a son and two daughters.

Audrey's first son Michael (1958) has a son, and although her second son Robert (1961) has no children, he does live next door to George's old house in College Street. Audrey's only daughter Stella (1962), has a son and daughter.

Funeral of Miss Molly Clarke

THE funeral service for Miss Molly Vera Clarke, of 183, College Street, Nuneaton, was held at Coton Parish Church yesterday.

Miss Clark, aged 42, was employed as a civilian clerk at Nuneaton Police Headquarters until her death. She died in the George Eliot Hospital on Saturday. The service was conducted by the Vicar, the Rev R. R. P. Rigby.

Principal mourners were: Mr and Mrs H. J. Sidwell (sister and brother-in-law); Mr and Mrs T. Sheehan (sister and brother-in-law); Mrs M. Pegg (aunt); Mr W. W. Daulman (cousin).

Representing Warwickshire Constabulary: J. Stanley (Assistant Chief Constable); Supt. A. W. Spooner; Det. Supt. J. H. Dodridge; Chief Inspr. C. G. Taylor; Inspr. T. L. Crawford; and many other members of the Nuneaton Police Division including members of the female civilian staff.

Floral tributes were received from: Dad, Norah and Harry, Audrey and Tommy; David and Michael; Auntie May and Auntie Flo; Auntie Charlotte and Uncle Arthur; Auntie Flo, Uncle Sid, Sid and Marion; Mabel and Jack, Bill and Winnie; Rene and family (Ilford); Charles and Doreen; Marion, Ivor and Delphine; Uncle Joe and family; Bob and Myrtle; Mr and Mrs Stanley; Jack and Edith Holbrook; Chief Constable and all Ranks, Warwickshire Constabulary; Nuneaton Division, Warwickshire Constabulary; Colleagues, Nuneaton Police; Lance Brian, Wib, and Roger (ex-Police Cadets); Mr and Mrs Royce; Mr and Mrs Grimes and Marjorie; Mr and Mrs Siers and Mr and Mrs Wykes; Mr and Mrs Leedham; Hilda and Bert Bucknall; Friends and neighbours (College Street); Mr and Mrs Ward; George and Nellie Rymell; Mr and Mrs G. Sidwell (Deacon Street); Committee and Members (Nuneaton Conservative Club).

Mr G. L. Clarke is mourned

THE funeral of Mr George L. Clarke, of 183 College Street, Nuneaton, took place at Chilvers Coton Church.

The Rev R. R. P. Rigby officiated.

The mourners were: Mr and Mrs H. J. Sidwell (daughter and son-in-law), Mr and Mrs T. Sheehan (daughter and son-in-law), Mrs M. Pegg (sister), and Mr T. O. Betteridge (grandson).

Wreaths were sent by: Family cross from Norah and Harry, Audrey and Tommy; Tommy, David and Michael (grandsons); Albert, Ethel and family; Sister Flo and family (Ilford); Sister May; Sid, Flo, Sid and Marion; Charlotte, Arthur and Lizzie; Bill, Winifred, Mabel and Jack; Charles and Doreen; Mr and Mrs Royce and Ann; Mr and Mrs Grimes and Marjorie; Mr and Mrs Leedham; Mr and Mrs Wykes and Mr and Mrs Siers; Mr and Mrs Ward; Friends and neighbours of College Street.

Index

311

A final word

Aunty May was a terrific character, warm and funny, with no self-consciousness at all. I rarely saw her without a hat. In her later years she was housekeeper to Tut Moore (an ex-Mayor of Nuneaton) and lived in his house on Manor Court Road. I remember her serving up sherry trifle after tea, using a big serving spoon that made that luscious sucking 'spock' sound as it came up out of the bowl. She was serving it in individual dishes, but dropped one, and it fell upside down on the kitchen floor. Without hesitation, she spooned it back in the dish, saying with a wink "That one's for Mr. Moore."

In searching through the family photographs we rediscovered this wonderful picture of her. How many people can say "...and that's my Aunty May holding the lion ?." Yes, it's taken at a British seaside resort, and yes, it's a real live lion.

DS